# REAL ESTATE INVESTING

## A Complete Guide To Making Money In Real Estate In Your Home Town

This book is an easy, step-by-step system, if followed, will allow you to reach your goal of Financial Freedom for you and your loved ones. This system has been successfully followed by thousand of people just like you....and you are next!

Within these covers you will discover:
- How to get the good deals
- How to ensure you're not offering too much
- How to lock in your profit when you buy (not when you sell!)
- How to confidently estimate repairs
- How to successfully run a real estate investment from the innitial offer to your bank account

This book is a system designed for you to use over and over again in your real estate business. It is complete with all of the forms that -- if used each and every time you do a deal -- will almost guarantee you success. Not only will this system help you become successful, but it will also allow you to build your business to the level that you want it to be, at a much faster and profitable pace than if you were to do this business like I did, by trial and error.

CreativeSuccessAlliance.com
100 Weymouth St. Rockland, MA 02370
781-878-7114

ISBN 978-0-615-46

9 780615 465371

# REAL ESTATE INVESTING

## A Complete Guide to Making Money in Real Estate in Your Home Town

## David Lindahl

*For general information on our other products and services, please contact our Customer Care Department at 781-878-7114.*

*Lindahl, David*
*Real Estate Investing - A Complete Guide to Making Money in Real Estate in Your Home Town*

*ISBN  978-0-615-46537-1*

To Get the Forms for This Book and A Free Bonus Gift visit
www.FormsForBook.com

*To All Those Looking To Improve Their Lives, This Book Is Dedicated To You*

# Table of Contents

To Get the Forms for This Book and A Free Bonus Gift visit
www.FormsForBook.com

To Get the Forms for This Book and A Free Bonus Gift visit
www.FormsForBook.com

## 8) Property Inspection and How to Determine Cost................................ 126

To Get the Forms for This Book and A Free Bonus Gift visit
www.FormsForBook.com

To Get the Forms for This Book and A Free Bonus Gift visit
www.FormsForBook.com

# *Chapter 1*

# **Introduction**

Congratulations and welcome to Real Estate Investing: A Complete Guide To Making Money In Real Estate In Your Home Town, you made a wise decision to invest in this book and invest in yourself!

This book will show you how to put money in your pocket by investing in real estate in your back yard today!

There has never been a better time to be investing in real estate than right now....as a matter of fact, it is always a good time to be investing in real estate regardless of what the national economy is doing and what your local economy is doing.

With the information you will discover between these pages you could put $5,000, $10,000, $15,000, to $50,000 in your pocket in a very short period of time...in most cases less than thirty days and then you'll be able to duplicate those results with over and over again!

It's A System.....

What you have in your hands is a system, a system that was created by a crazy kid who spent too long in a rock and roll band and when he finally smartened up and decided to do something with his life, he got involved in real estate and changed his life forever.

I happen to be that kid and at the writing of this book, I own over 7,000 real estate units and my portfolio continues to grow and so will yours...if you read this book in its entirety and take action with the knowledge you are about to gain.

You're On A Road To Discovery....

To Get the Forms for This Book and A Free Bonus Gift visit
www.FormsForBook.com

Between these pages, you'll discover how to find deals that are hidden right now in your back yard. Deals that you pass by every single day. Deals that you will learn to recognize very easily now that you are about to embark on the secret of real estate investing.

Your also going to discover ways to get motivated sellers to call you directly to sell you their houses at a discount. Imagine your phone rings, you pick it up, on the other line is a person who for some reason, needs to sell their house quickly, so quickly they are willing to sell it to you at a big profit.....$20 - 50,000 profit. You make an appointment to see the property, the deal is what you think it is. You put it under contract and then you put a simple add in the classified section of you newspaper "Motivated Seller Needs To Sell Quickly - Cash Buyers Only".

The ad runs, your phone begins to ring off the hook with motivated buyers looking to buy the house. You take their names, numbers and ask them for proof of funds before you bring them over to the property.

Those who give you the information and qualify meet you at the property, all at the same time. You show them the property (in your contract, the seller agrees to allow you to show the property as long as you give them a 48 hour notice). After the showing, you talk to the investors outside, you let them know that it's first come, first serve. Whoever gives you your assignment fee (explained later in the book) gets the deal.

You figured if you sold this house to an end buyer and waited the sixty to ninety days to close, you would have made a profit of $50,000, but you didn't want to wait, you wanted....or needed money now!

So you decided to wholesale the property to another investor in return for an assignment fee of $10,000. The investors gives you the certified check for $10,000, you assign the contract to the investor and now you are as happy as a clam (hey, I'm from New England!) and just like your Saturday night dates, you want to do it again and again and again.....and you can, because you were smart enough to invest in a book like this and to learn from someone who has over seventeen years experience in the real estate game. Again, I congratulate you!

Analyzing Deals Will Set You Free

To Get the Forms for This Book and A Free Bonus Gift visit
www.FormsForBook.com

This book is a system; this system will show you how to analyze the deals to make sure you are getting in a good deal every time. We make money when we buy real estate; we realize the money when we sell. That's a very important sentence, you must buy right to put money in your pocket when you sell.

You must get good at analyzing deals and I will take you step by step through that process.

Analyzing deals consists of knowing what the after repaired value is on a property, knowing how to estimate the cost of any repairs that need to be done to the property and also knowing the work flow that should take place on a property should you decide to see the deal through to the end and not wholesale it.

Can We Talk About Your Business?

Let me take a minute and talk about your real estate business. If you need money right now, the easiest way to get it is to wholesale a property. Then you can use that money to pay off some bills, make a mortgage or a car payment or whatever else you need to do to get your head above water.

Perhaps it will take a couple of deals to get your head above water but once your head is above water, it's time to consider holding these deals through to the end buyer. What I mean is, buy the property, do the minor repairs that are needed and then remarket the property to an end buyer.

When you do this, you make the most amount of money and you really start to create large wealth for you and your loved ones. After you have done this a few times, you then must consider holding on to some properties for cash flow and appreciation.

Cash Flow And Appreciation? Forward Thinking.....

We are getting ahead of ourselves here but you don't want to hold single family properties for cash flow and appreciation, you want multi-family properties.

I know what you're thinking....but Dave, I don't want to be a landlord, I don't want tenants....you know what I say to that? If you do become a landlord and you do deal with tenants....I will track you down and beat you!!!

I will show you how to hire good quality management companies to manage your properties so you sole function is to cash checks and do deals....but that is a subject for another one of my books Multi-Family Millions which you can get easily on Amazon.com

The Estimating Process Will Lock In Your Profits

In this book, I will spend a lot of time on the estimating process because this is where so many investors lose money. They lose money because they underestimate the repairs of a property.

They underestimate the repairs because they don't know all of the repairs to look for. The repairs the miss are the ones that cost them money. They are the ones that keep them from cashing bigger checks at closing.

This will not happen to you as long as you follow the checklists I provide for you...it's a system!

The next step will be to put in an offer. After you analyze the deal, you will know what you need to pay for it, your maximum allowable offer, in order to make the amount of money you want to make on the deal. But where do you start with the offer process?

You don't want to pay more than you have to for the property, each dollar you save when you are buying the property is another dollar you put in your pocket when you sell the property.

Insult The Seller?

And you certainly don't want to insult the seller. Giving the seller a low ball offer on a good deal risks that seller not only not countering your offer but also refusing another offer from you.

This is called negotiating and I will give you some key strategies to negotiating the deal so you can make the very best deal for yourself and have the seller thanking you for doing business with you!

Next you close on the deal and either wholesale it or keep if for the end buyer. When you start keeping deals for the end buyer, you will start following the repair checklists

Your Promise To Me

Now here is your big promise to me....you will not do the repairs on your own properties!!! You will hire other people to do those repairs, you factored it into the deal anyway!, so you continue to do what you will get really good at doing; marketing for new deals and negotiating with sellers...and watching your bank account grow!

Finally, I will give you strategies to use to sell your properties. There are a lot of little tricks to use to sell your properties to get top dollar, we'll discuss those so your deals fly off the shelf to be replaced by the next deal that is going to represent another check that is going to go into your pocket.

Putting it All Together

When you put these strategies together, you will get some awesome results. In my seventeen plus years of investing I've lost track of the total number of properties that I have either wholesaled or flipped but let me share with you some of the results I have gotten.

As I said, I'm still investing in real estate today, I never stopped investing for the last seventeen years and I will probably continue to invest to my dying days. I'm currently working on a property that is a four bedroom colonial home with an in law apartment. I bought the property for $319,000 and plan to put $22,000 worth of work in the property.

It needs some carpet, interior and exterior paint, refinishing of some hardwood floors, some new lighting and windows. I will do none of the work myself and when it's complete, the property should sell for $525,000.

That's $341000 going into the deal, probably another $8,000 in miscellaneous costs which brings us up to $349,000. That's a profit of $184,000!

How did I get such a good deal? Foreclosure. Bank wanted to sell quickly.

Here is the best part. We had a neighbor come by the other day and say they had their house under agreement and wanted to buy our house as is but didn't want to pay anymore than $450,000. That's a profit of $99,000....no wait, we wouldn't have to do any work so we save the $22,000 in repairs and most of the miscellaneous costs, lets add another $7,000 to the profits....$29,000 + $99,000 = $128,000! Not bad for getting into the real estate game!!

$172,000 Flipping A Deal?

A student of mine, Rick Chafee decided that he would get into the game, He got the opportunity to buy two multifamily properties, a 10 unit and a 12 unit. At the time, he had no desire to hold on to multifamily properties, I say at the time because now he owns several hundred units and enjoys those cash flow checks coming in each month!

He decided to wholesale these two properties to a buyer who wanted to hold them for the cash flow. Rick was able to pocket a check for $170,000 and his buyer was happy as heck because Rick gave him a "good deal" on the properties!!

You might be thinking, why would anyone sell a property with that much equity or in the first example I gave you, why wouldn't the seller just put the ad in the paper themselves and sell it to an end buyer. Well, the reason is.....I don't know, but it happens every day and I learned to stop asking why and accept the fact that motivated sellers are motivated sellers and for whatever reason they need to sell, they need and want to sell know and if you are prepared, you will be getting great deals too.

To Get the Forms for This Book and A Free Bonus Gift visit
www.FormsForBook.com

Singles and Home Runs

The few examples I've given you so far have very large profit margins and although these deals are not unusual, they are what we call "homeruns"....I love watching my Boston Red Sox hit homeruns … especially against the Yankees!!

Homeruns are great but the majority of games are won by singles and doubles. In real estate, you want to be hitting a lot of "singles" and "doubles", these are you bread and butter deals. These are the deals that put between $5,000 and $30,000 in your bank account on a regular basis.

The system you are about to learn will not only show you how to get a hold of a few home runs every now and then but also how to hit singles and doubles on a regular basis. It has changed the lives of thousands of people like Val Harper.

How Did Val Make $53,000?

Val was a real estate agent when we first met. She had spent her days making other people money buying and selling real estate. She finally got tired of seeing her clients cashing big check and decided to take the next step and educate herself and do her first real investment deal.

She bought herself a three bedroom ranch, put some work into the property, not much but the important stuff like updating the kitchen and baths. When she sold the property she skipped her way from the closing table down to the bank and deposited a $53,000 check into her bank account.

These are stories of people who are just like you who took their time, learned a system, took action and implemented that system....now they are living the lives they were born to live.

My Story

But what about me, you're probably wondering how I started and why I am qualified to be your mentor. Well......this is the story....

To Get the Forms for This Book and A Free Bonus Gift visit
www.FormsForBook.com

I was twenty six years old, I had been in a rock and roll band for almost ten years, doing all of those things you hear rock and roller doing. Yes those were crazy times and I had a lot of fun. I tried like heck to make it in rock and roll but it just wasn't going to happen.

The Next Mick Jagger

I was the lead vocals and I saw myself as the next Mick Jaggar, I had the moves, my voice wasn't great but I could grab any crowd by the throat and bring them for a two hour ride of merriment, joy and sorrow. By the time the show was over, we were one and we would be exhausted, I gave them everything I had and they returned my commitment by giving me every ounce of their energy. Together we create experiences.

But alas, I was smart enough to realize that the dream would not go on and it was time to smarten up, make some money and start living a "normal" life....much to the joy of my mother!

What Is Normal?

By the way, I put "normal" in parenthesis because, does anyone really know what normal is? I certainly don't but it seems to go hand in hand with boring and the last thing I have lived is a boring life and when you start your journey into this chapter of you life, you will be able to challenge "normal" yourself!

In The Beginning...

So I started a landscaping company. I was told if you ever want to make serious money, you either have to sell something or you have to own it. I decided to own my own landscaping company.

I went neighborhood to neighborhood looking for anyone who had high grass and I knocked on their doors and asked them if I could mow their lawns. I got forty one accounts that first year and things were going pretty good until the winter came and everything froze.

In the winter, there were no lawns to mow, no holes to dig and no income coming in. In the wintertime I struggled. I did all kinds of odd jobs

To Get the Forms for This Book and A Free Bonus Gift visit
www.FormsForBook.com

just to get by. I sold memberships for BJ's Wholesale Club and Costco's, I did a lot snow plowing. I did anything I had to do to get by until the springtime came.

## The Big Break

Then one day I got a phone call from a friend of mine who worked for a local bank. The bank had foreclosed on a property and needed someone to do the work on the property so they could resell it.

My friend asked me if I wanted the job. I said "absolutely", I would have done anything to get money to come into my one bedroom apartment, but I had a problem. I didn't know how to do the work; I didn't even know how to bid the job!

## What Would You Do If You Didn't Know What You Didn't Know?

So I thought of all the people I know and asked the those who knew how to bid jobs to help me bid and when I won the job, I asked all the people who knew how to do the work to help me do the work. And when I couldn't find anyone who knew how to do the work, I learned how to hire contractors to do the work.

And it worked. I was able to get that first deal done, the bank liked the work, they were able to resell it quickly and they asked me to bid a second one and I did that job and then another and another and then I started noticing something.

## Hmmmm, Opportunity

I started noticing that there people who were buying these properties from the bank, flipping them and making 10, 20 and 30,000 dollars on the flip.
It was then I realized I was on the wrong side of the transaction. I needed to learn to do what they were doing so I could get some of those paydays myself.

So I started searching for ways to make money in real estate. I bought all kinds of books and tapes, went to all kinds of seminars and I collected a good library of information but I always felt there was something missing. I felt I had just enough know how to get started but not enough to actually do a deal and this was very frustrating.

Problems, Problems, Problems

I was also dealing with a lot of fear. Fear of doing my first deal, fear of screwing up my first deal, fear of doing the wrong analysis, fear of failure, fear of success, fear, fear, fear......

And I had another problem, I had no money. How could I buy a house if I didn't have any money? I had heard of people buying properties with no money down but could it work for me and if it could, how?

It took me a long time to figure things out. Every time I went to a different seminar, I would hear a different method of investing in real estate and why that method was the one to use.

I must admit, I was easily sold on all of these techniques but I couldn't seem to get one to work. All I wanted was one to work so I could do my first deal and cash my first check and then do it again and again.

The Breakthrough

My breakthrough came when I got a mentor. My mentor explained to me the basic foundation of every real estate deal. He explained to me how to do deal without any money coming from my pocket. He explained to me how to analyze deals very conservatively so I would make money on any deal that qualified using these methods.

I followed what he said and it worked. After nine months of frustration, I finally did my fist deal. Within the next three months I had three more, within nine months I had eleven deals. I was rolling. My bank account was starting to fill up. I started getting monthly cash flow checks from properties that I held long term. I started weaning better closes, taking vacations, driving a better car but more importantly, I was able to give back to my family first and then my community.

To Get the Forms for This Book and A Free Bonus Gift visit
www.FormsForBook.com

The crazy kid in the rock and roll band had finally turned his life around and was not only making money but making a difference in other people's lives.

Since then i have not looked back. I've continued to grow my real estate portfolio. I've continued to spend more time with my family and friends and I've continued to give back to my community.

I'm living a fulfilled life and I have trained tens of thousands of students all around North America and the world...and your next!!

Why Oh Why Can't I

I've been educating now for over seven years and I have not only heard every excuse there is for people who say they can't do real estate but I've also lived those excuses myself until I got off my butt and stopped kidding myself.

I used to think that you needed money to invest in real estate. I quickly learned that wasn't true. You can wholesale deals, you can use hard money, private money and creative seller financing.

I Have No Time!

I've heard people tell me they don't have time to do real estate. I used to think the same thing until I realized it takes one half hour a day for four days a week...that is literally two hours a week to get started investing in real estate. If you can't find four half hour sessions per week, you are destined to live the life of those people who sit on the side of the road repeating the words "I should have, I could have...."

Think about it, you're reading this book because you want to change your life, your circumstances and it takes a commitment. Not a very big commitment but a commitment. If you really think about it, when things start really going well with your real estate investing, you will be a full time investor, your time will your own and you'll be living your life on your terms....if that's what you want, you can have it but I need a small commitment from you. The first being, read this entire book, the second being, taking action.

If you will do those two small things for me, I promise you, the information you are about to discover will change your life.

I Have No Support!

I've heard people say, I'd love to invest in real estate but I don't have any support from my family and friends. Neither did I. My father kept telling me, if I invest in real estate I'm going to "go down"...."dooooooowwwwwwnnnnnnnnn". He made me so nervous; I stopped talking to him about investing in real estate. If I listened to all the naysayers, I wouldn't own over 7,000 units right now!

I've heard people say, "Oh, nothing ever works out for me". Just by them saying that, they are ensuring that nothing will ever work out for them!! You've got to have a positive attitude. Life is all about attitude and you can control your attitude, that's the great thing about it. If you decide that life sucks...it sucks. If you decide that life is going to be good, it's going to be good!

You get to decide how your day is going to go, most people live by allowing other people control their attitudes and they never figure out they have a choice....what a pity, a life lost in the abyss.

I'm Not Smart Enough!

Some people think they aren't smart enough to do real estate. Hey, none of us are born with the ability to buy and sell real estate but most of us can follow a system. if you can follow a system, you can do real estate. It's a simple, step by step system, all you have to do is follow the steps and you can't help but be successful and then you will be the envy of all your friends, family and neighbors....

What's your reason for not being able to do real estate? I'll bet you a free admission to my Real Estate Academy Boot Camp, a $3,000 value, that you can't call my office, talk with one of my business strategist and give them a reason you can't do real estate that they haven't helped another student to successfully overcome. I challenge you, call the office

To Get the Forms for This Book and A Free Bonus Gift visit
www.FormsForBook.com

781 878 7114, set up an appointment and give it your best shot. Be prepared to be given a step by step solution to put your next check in your pocket....and quickly!

Your Turn

Seventeen years ago, it was my turn. A crazy kid from a rock and roll band who has a lot less brain cells than he had before he entered the band, wanted a better life. He started investing in real estate; he created a step by step system that allowed him to get into his first deal and into thousands of deals after that.

In doing so, he created a life for him and his family that he never imagined could exist and it does because he took action.

Now it's your turn. Time to overcome the excuses, time to seize the opportunity that is in front of you, time to change yours and your family's life for the better and it all starts with the turning of the pages of this book.....so without further ado.....let's start your journey!

To Get the Forms for This Book and A Free Bonus Gift visit
www.FormsForBook.com

# Chapter 2

# Goal Setting

The most successful people I know are all goal setters. They sit down and vision where they want to be, decide how long they want it to take them to get there, and write up a plan and stick to it until they have reached their goal.

After they reach that goal, they set another, then another. If you have ever wondered what it takes to be successful, this is one of the most important -- if not <u>the</u> most important -- attributes of a successful person.

There is a famous study done about the graduating class of 1954 from Harvard University. If you haven't already heard about it, I'm going to tell you about the results. If you have heard about it, I'm going to go over it again, because it is that important.

The students were interviewed in the mid 1980s and were asked, among other things, if they consistently wrote down their goals. Only three percent had made it a habit of writing down and reviewing their goals. As it turned out, that three percent were far wealthier than the other 97 percent of the class. As a matter of fact, that three percent had obtained 87 percent of the wealth of that entire class had generated. Isn't that amazing?! **That** is the power of goal setting.

The fastest way to obtain anything that you want from life, whether it is to drive a new car, acquire more money, buy more houses, or take longer vacations, is to have written goals.

A goal must be written. If it's still in your head, it's just a dream. And while dreams are good, goals will make you wealthy.

When you write your dream (your vision) down on paper, it instantly becomes a goal. A funny thing happens when you commit a goal to writing. Your subconscious mind, as if on command, starts directing your conscious mind toward achieving that goal. Even though you may

To Get the Forms for This Book and A Free Bonus Gift visit
www.FormsForBook.com

not realize it, your mind is now working like a stealth fighter. It is secretly directing you towards your goals. It's taking all of your life choices and aiming your future actions to the fulfillment of your goals.

In order for a goal to be effective, it must be measurable. This means that you must be specific as to what you want. For example, writing down, "My goal is to be rich," is not the correct way to write a goal. Everybody wants to be rich, but being rich means something different to each and every one of us. You need to put your definition of rich in your goal. Here is the right way to write that goal:

"I want to earn $1 million dollars."

All right! Now we have a specific, measurable goal. The next thing you need to do is give your goal a deadline. You need something to push you along, something that you can measure your progress against. If you say that you want to earn one million dollars and you finally reach one million dollars when you are 80 years old, have you really reached your goal? No! You want that money earlier so that you can enjoy it. You want it soon! So write it down.

"I want to earn $1 million dollars by January 1, 20__."

O.K., now we're getting somewhere. There is just one more step that you have to take to have a complete goal. You must write your goal in the present tense, as if it's already here and it is already happening. It looks like this:

"On January 1, 20__, I am worth $1 million dollars."

That's it! You need to see yourself already accomplishing your goal. You need to live it inside of your mind and see what that money will do for you. Feel the security it gives you and your family, see the dream vacation that you will be taking your wife or husband on, see what type of house that money will buy for you.

This is getting you emotionally attached to your goal, and this is the most powerful step in goal setting. When you become emotionally involved in your goals -- when your reasons for achieving these goals are constantly reviewed by you and ingrained in you -- and you associate this goal with an emotional benefit, you will achieve it.

Your written goal now looks like this:

"On January 1, 2004, I am worth $1 million dollars. Having this money gives me the security of knowing that I can give my children a college education, my partner and I no longer worry about our bills, I can take my partner on any dream vacation that he/she wants to go on, and we live in the house that we've always talked about."

That's it, you're hooked! Every one of your goals should be written like this. Then, after you write them down, put them in a spot where you can see them and read them every day. This is important. Don't hide them away! The best time to read your goals is either in the morning when you first wake up or right before you go to bed.

When you first wake up and are just coming out of sleep, your subconscious mind is still very active. When you read your goals at this time, they will be easily accepted into your subconscious. That's where you want them, working in your subconscious like a stealth fighter.

When you read them right before you go to sleep, your subconscious mind has all night to plot and plan ways to accomplish them. A lot of times you will wake up with a great new idea of how to get you closer to your goal. This is your subconscious at work. It's always working, it never sleeps.

To achieve your goals, you must, absolutely must, believe that you can.

The phrase "Fake it until you make it" is true. You not only have to envision your goal, but you have also got to start living it as if you have already attained it. It's a proven fact that your mind can't tell the difference between reality and fantasy, so if you envision your goal and act like you are already there, your mind will assume that this is the norm and you will achieve the goal that much faster.

To Get the Forms for This Book and A Free Bonus Gift visit
www.FormsForBook.com

Have you ever read the book *Think and Grow Rich* by Napolean Hill? If you haven't you should. In the book, Hill talks about a "secret" throughout the entire book. And he tells you that if you can figure out the secret you can become richer than your wildest dreams. Well, the secret is to believe from the bottom of your heart that you already are what you want to be, and you will become it.

To give you an example of how this came about in my life, about one year into my construction business, I decided that I was going to also be a successful real estate investor. I envisioned myself owning many pieces of real estate, I saw myself driving in a fine car and wearing a business suit (because at that time I thought all successful real estate investors wore suits). Little did I know!

Well I started wearing a two-piece suit into the office. The first day my secretary asked me what the big occasion was. I told her that I'd decided that this is the way that I was going to dress from now on when I didn't have to be on a job site. She thought I was crazy.

Well, I continued to change into a two-piece suit every time I went into the office (the office was above my garage at my house!). And each time I bought and sold another piece of property, I rewarded myself with another suit.

Next thing you know, I have a closet full of suits, a bank account full of money and more properties than a monopoly board. All because I lived my vision before I got there (my vision included more than just the two piece suit...and I lived it all way before I got there).

You know what else is funny? When I went out in public wearing that suit instead of jeans and a T-shirt, I was treated a whole lot differently. People started calling me sir. Clerks were more pleasant, and at a crowded counter I was usually one of the first to be waited on. My credibility went sky high.

It got to the point that I realized that whenever someone was rude to me or whenever I was treated badly or I was not taken seriously, I was usually underdressed.

To Get the Forms for This Book and A Free Bonus Gift visit
www.FormsForBook.com

Try it sometime. The next time you go out shopping either at the grocery store or at the mall, wear a suit or some very nice casual clothes. Notice how you are treated. Also notice the way your own self-esteem rises. Notice how good you feel about yourself.

You know it's true that people want to do business with successful people. If you're not successful yet, dress as if you are. You'll get there. Then you can dress however you want!

Let me share with you my experience with goal setting. When I was 30 years old I lived in a three-room apartment. I had been in a rock-and-roll band for 10 years and decided that now was the time to get serious about life. Now was the time to make some money.

I started a landscape company, basically knocking on people's doors that had tall grass in their yard. I was searching for a way to get rich quick. I started reading everything I could but nothing seemed to click.

Then I got a hold of Earl Nightingale's "Lead the Field" tape set. Those tapes changed my life! I was referred to another tape set that taught me how to set my goals. I listened to a lot of the same information that I am telling you now and sat down and wrote out my one-, three-, and six-month goals, as well as my one-, five-, 10-, 15- and 20-year goals. I did this because the speaker told me to and I did it because I wanted to be successful. It took a while but I did it. I wrote them down and reviewed them often.

Within two years I had reached most of my five-year goals, and within five years I had reached most of my 15-year goals. That's the power of goal setting.

You don't have to start writing all of the goals the way I did (it certainly can't hurt), but you should write down your 30-day, six-month, and one-, three- and five-year goals.

Separate your goals into four major categories: financial goals, business goals, health goals and family goals.

To Get the Forms for This Book and A Free Bonus Gift visit
www.FormsForBook.com

O.K., now that you have your goals, you have to take it just one step further. You have to have a plan. It's great to realize what you want and when you want it. Now you've got to figure out how you're going to get it.

What you'll need to do is take every one of your goals and break them down into plans. There's an old saying, "Failing to plan is planning to fail." This is true. Whenever a builder builds a house, he first starts with a plan. The tallest skyscraper is begun with a plan. When you go on vacation, the first thing you do is plan. When you decide what you want in life, you've got to plan it out.

Let's take the goal of earning $1 million. You decide that you will earn this money through real estate investing. That's the first part of the plan. You figure that each time you go into a real estate transaction, whether it be buying rehabs or pretty houses, your profit is going to be $20,000 per house. That means that you are going to have to do 50 transactions to get to the $1 million ($1 million divided by $20,000 equals 50).

Now we know what we need to do, now we've got to create a plan to get those 50 houses. So you sit down and review all of the materials that you have read or listened to regarding real estate investing.

If your goal is to be a millionaire in five years (not unreasonable -- and neither is two years -- it just depends how motivated you are) that means that you've got to do 10 houses per year (50 divided by five equals 10). Taking that one step further, you will have to buy just under one house per month (12 months a year divided by ten equals .83). At this point you may be thinking, how am I going to buy one house per month? That's good, because that means you are planning.

To get one house per month, you need to find deals or attract deals to you. You do this by creating a marketing plan.

Your plan may look like this:

In order to attract 10 deals a year I will do the following: hand out five business cards per day; put an ad in the newspaper; read or listen to a new real estate investing book or course every two weeks (the more you learn the more you earn!); hand out flyers to targeted neighborhoods; establish relationships with realtors; put up bandit signs in my targeted towns; establish relationships with attorneys; attend at least one auction a week…

Now you've broken down your goal into a workable plan. That big goal of $1 million doesn't look so big now because you've broken it down into daily tasks.

Each day you will be working your plan that will get you to your goal. How do you eat an elephant? One bite at a time!

Most people won't take the time to do this. Most people are not successful. Success is a choice. Successful people do what unsuccessful people won't.

An oil tanker that is looking to make a 180-degree turn in the open ocean takes about two miles to complete the turn. A person learning how to set goals and plan for the first time in his or her life will take time to be effective at it. At times you will follow your plan to the "T." At other times, a few days or a week will go by and you will realize that you haven't been working your plan. That's O.K., as long as you realize what you are doing and get back to your plan. Just because you lose a few days here and there doesn't mean you're a failure. The only time you're a failure is when you quit. Keep going back to your plan and goals and, like that tanker in the open ocean, you will change the direction of your life.

The last thing that you should know about goal setting is to reward yourself when you reach your goals! Whether you've reached a small goal or a major goal, reward yourself. Write down a list of things that you would like to reward yourself with. Whether it be a suit, which I used to do, or a night out, weekend away…it doesn't matter what it is as long as it has meaning to you.

If you want to ensure your success, be a goal setter and a planner, then write to me and tell me how this has changed your life!

# My Goals
# (What I Am Achieving Now!)

## Business
List three goals related to your business

**1.**_____

**2.**_____

**3.**_____    _____

## Family
List three goals related to your family

**1.**_____

**2.**_____

**3.**_____    _____

## Financial
List three goals relating to income growth, savings, investments and retirement.

**1.**_____

**2.**_____

**3.**_____    _____

To Get the Forms for This Book and A Free Bonus Gift visit
www.FormsForBook.com

# Health

List three goals relating to exercise, diet and your overall health and well being.

**1.**_____

**2.**_____

**3.**_____

# Activities

| Activity/Function | Due Date | Comments |
|---|---|---|
|  |  |  |
|  |  |  |
|  |  |  |
|  |  |  |
|  |  |  |
|  |  |  |
|  |  |  |
|  |  |  |
|  |  |  |
|  |  |  |
|  |  |  |
|  |  |  |
|  |  |  |
|  |  |  |
|  |  |  |
|  |  |  |
|  |  |  |
|  |  |  |

To Get the Forms for This Book and A Free Bonus Gift visit
www.FormsForBook.com

## The I Knew I Could Do It, Goal Achiever's Rewards List

1) _____

2) _____

3) _____

4) _____

5) _____

6) _____

7) _____

8) _____

9) _____

10) _____

# Chapter 3
## Pre-Foreclosures/Auctions

Picture this in your mind: You lost your part-time job four months ago and you needed that money, along with what you earned on your full-time job to pay your mortgage. You can't seem to find another part-time job, and now you're hearing rumors of layoffs in your day job. You're already three months behind on your mortgage payments, your credit cards bills are starting to pile up, and you've just received a notice from the bank that they are going to foreclose on the house by the end of the month.

How did this happen? One minute, life is good and stress-free. The next minute, you find yourself in deep despair. Not only may you be without a job, but soon you may even lose the roof over your head. You never thought that **you** would ever be homeless, let alone penniless.

You've talked to your friends, relatives and anyone else who might be able to give you a hand, but no one has the extra cash that you need to bring your mortgage current. You've spoken to your bank regarding refinancing, but they do not like to refinance someone who is already behind on their payments. The priest at your church says that donations have been down lately, and he won't be able to help.

Bankruptcy is an option, but there must be a better way.

As you contemplate your dilemma, the mailman comes and drops off the day's mail. You notice a hand-addressed envelope. You don't recognize the return address, but it must be someone you know, because it's got a regular stamp on it.

When you open the envelope, the letter states that the person who sent it is a real estate investor, and he is interested in buying your house and getting you out of your financial troubles.

To Get the Forms for This Book and A Free Bonus Gift visit
www.FormsForBook.com

By selling your house, you will be able to get cash for the equity that you have in it. Cash that you can use to get yourself an apartment or even buy yourself another house, when you get your financial situation straightened out.

The letter also informs you that by selling your house, you will avoid the foreclosure and bankruptcy process, thereby doing less damage to your credit rating. And the less damage you do to your credit rating, the easier it will be to buy your next house when you are ready.

At last! A light at the end of this long, dark tunnel. You pick up the phone and dial the number. You are saved!

## Give Me a Hungry, Starving Crowd…

Is this a motivated seller? You bet it is! And there are plenty of motivated sellers just like this person, in the same situation, facing foreclosure with seemingly no way out. That is the beauty of the pre-foreclosure market. Not only do you have very motivated sellers, but you also have an almost endless supply of leads to contact these people.

Where do you find the leads? First, you must understand the foreclosure process. When an individual gets behind on their mortgage, the lending institution's recourse is to foreclose on the property and take possession. Since the property was put up as collateral for the mortgage, this is the bank's right. As a matter of fact, when you sign a mortgage for a property, inside that document you are agreeing that if you do not make your payments, you the give the bank the authority to take back the property.

## The Soldiers and Sailors Act

Although they have the authority to do so, the bank must follow a certain procedure. The first thing they must do is to comply with the "Soldiers and Sailors Act". In 1940, the federal government passed a law that stated that no lending institution could foreclose on a property until it publicly advertised its intentions. Inside that advertisement, they asked the public if anyone knew if persons being foreclosed on were in one of the branches of the military service, to please contact the lending institution. Inside the advertisement would be a date that the bank would have to be contacted by, in order to stop the foreclosure proceedings.

This law was enacted to protect the men and women who were in the military, fighting World War II. At the beginning of the war, with no way to make their mortgage payments from the battlefields, some of our soldiers came home to find that somebody else was living in their house. While they were away, the bank had foreclosed on them for lack of payments.

What irony! This man has just come back from the bloody fields of Normandy, risking his life for the country he loves. Risking his life so that the banking institution that holds his mortgage would be protected from the ravages of Hitler's machine. And he comes home victorious! Only to find out that his home has been taken away from him by the people he so valiantly fought to protect.

This is why Congress passed the Soldiers and Sailors Act. Most lending institutions comply with this act by advertising in the local paper or the financial paper where the property is located.

They also must file at the local courthouse of their intention to foreclose.

If no one responds by the date on the notice, then the foreclosure goes into the final step. The lending institution must give public notice at least three times of its intentions to hold a foreclosure auction, the date and time of the auction, and where the auction will take place.

The auction usually takes place at either the courthouse steps or on the sidewalk in front of the property.

The homeowner has right up until the time of the auction to pay off any and all delinquencies. If they do this, they will bring the mortgage current and the auction will be called off.

Now that you know how the procedure works, the best time to contact the homeowner is when the first public notice comes out, in compliance with the Soldiers and Sailors Act.

You will find these public notices in the legal section of your newspaper, or in your local legal newspaper. Check them every day, and every day you will get new leads. You can also get this information from your local courthouse, though it is much easier and less time consuming to get them from the newspapers.

Each city has a local financial newspaper that comes out weekly; in our area it is called the Banker and Tradesman. You will find all of the Soldiers and Sailors announcements for a much wider area in these publications, because they cover numerous counties. They get their information directly from the courthouse.

There are also services that you can subscribe to, that will e-mail or mail you the current list of people in foreclosure for the areas that you want. These services will charge you either monthly or annually for the subscription. The prices can range from $20 a month, to a yearly subscription of $249 or higher.

## The Best Source for Pre-Foreclosure Information

Of all of the sources of information that were just mentioned, the best source is your local newspaper. The reason they are the best is because of timing. You want to contact these people as soon as possible; if you can, you want to be the first one in the door. There are other people

> ▶ *Tactical Tip...* ◀   **The best source for foreclosure leads is your local newspaper. The reason they are the best is because of timing. You want to contact these people as soon as possible; if you can, you want to be the first one in the door.**

who have discovered how lucrative the pre-foreclosure market is, and you will be competing with them.

Not only will you be competing with other investors, but attorneys also contact pre-foreclosures to offer their bankruptcy services. Mortgage companies will contact a pre-foreclosure if there is a lot of equity in the property, because they may be willing to refinance. This is why you want to make contact as soon as possible. If you take your time, you'll be losing out on some very good deals.

The newspapers are best because you get the public notice the first time it appears in public. You can literally be in contact with these people that afternoon.

The courthouse is good and you may get a head start on your competition by seeing the filing before it is on public notice, since it has to be filed before it is advertised. The problem is, depending how far the courthouse is away from your house and how busy your schedule is, the chances of you getting there every day is pretty slim. By the time you do get over there, somebody else may already have grabbed the deal.

The local financial papers and the foreclosure services usually have a two- to three-week lag time from when the filing takes place in the courthouse, and when it is published in their paper or service. Because of this, if you are in a market where the competition is stiff, that two- to three-week lag time is going to be too long.

## Three Ways to Make Contact

There are three different ways that you can make contact to a pre-foreclosure: You can call them, go to their house, or send them a letter. You may want to do each one.

When you first see a public notice for a pre-foreclosure that you are interested in, try to look up their number and call them. About 60 percent of the time, their number is unlisted. Since they have not been paying their bills, they are tired of the bill collectors calling, so they changed their number to an unlisted number.

To Get the Forms for This Book and A Free Bonus Gift visit
www.FormsForBook.com

If you cannot get them by phone and are still really interested in the property, you should go over and knock on the door. Be dressed nicely, and have a copy of the public notice with you. Let them know that their home is now due to be foreclosed on and you would like to help them out of this terrible situation.

Sometimes they will not even be aware that they were advertised in the legal section of the paper under the Soldiers and Sailors act until you tell them. Sometimes one of the parties, either the husband or wife, didn't even know that they were behind on their payments, because the other one had been hiding these facts from them. So be prepared for some surprises.

After introducing yourself, let them know that you would like to try to help them out of their financial situation. Then proceed to get all of the background information that you would need to construct an offer.

When working with pre-foreclosures, you should actually try to help the people out of their financial situation. If you can find a way to keep them in the house, keep them in the house.

## *Income/Expense Worksheet*

The first thing I do when I sit down with a new client, after I build rapport and show them my credibility kit (the kit is explained latter in the chapter), is to gather information. I explain to them that I want to help them stay in their house, and need some information that I am going to use to negotiate with the bank.

I ask permission to gather the information (always ask for permission), and then I pull out my Income/Expense worksheet and start filling in the blanks. I write down all of their income, all of their debt and all the cash outflows.

Their cash outflows are important, because people spend a lot of money on everyday things that they need to have in order to survive, such as electricity, food, and gas.

I then subtract the debt and outflows from the income, and determine if they have a cash surplus or a cash deficit.

If there is a cash surplus, I'll use this amount when negotiating with the bank. However, more often than not, there is a cash deficit. Most of the time, the homeowners didn't even know it until you showed them. Sure, they probably had an idea of their situation, but most of these people are in denial. This is probably the first time that they actually sat down and looked at the exact numbers.

Be prepared--I have had quite a few people break down and start crying. It is now that they finally realize that they cannot stay in the house. They simply can't afford it.

Now you have just set yourself up in the perfect position to be the one to buy their house and **help them** to make a fresh, new start (by buying their house, preventing a foreclosure on their credit, and giving them some cash to use to rebuild their lives).

## Creating Win/Win Situations by Helping Them Stay in Their Home

There are several things you can do to help them stay in the house. You could call their bank and negotiate a "workout" plan. Usually the bank divides the arrearage (amount of money owed) into 12, and adds that to their regular monthly mortgage payments. At the end of 12 months, they are caught up. While they are in "workout," they must make every payment. If they miss one, they go right back into the foreclosure process, and in most cases the bank will not do a workout plan a second time.

You may know of a lender who would either lend them the money to make up their back payments, or would refinance the entire first mortgage to bring them current.

If the homeowner knows that you are working in their best interest to keep them in the house, you will separate yourself from everyone else who has made contact with them, and whose only intention is to profit in some way from their unfortunate situation.

To Get the Forms for This Book and A Free Bonus Gift visit
www.FormsForBook.com

After you have exhausted all possibilities of them staying in the house and there is no other solution, then the next logical step is for you to help them get out of the situation by getting them out of the house. Of course, you do this by creating a win/win situation, and by buying the house.

You may find yourself helping many people stay in their houses, and you may think that this is counter-productive to what your goal is--to make money and buy the houses. It isn't.

First, only a very small percentage of people actually end up staying in their house.

Any time you help someone stay in their home, you become their hero and a friend for life. They will let everyone know what you did, how you helped them, and what a great guy or gal you are. They will always have their radar on, and when they hear of someone that is in trouble, they will refer them to you.

After you have helped them stay in their house, ask them to write you a referral letter, stating how desperate they were until you showed up on the scene. Ask them to write about your character, your honesty, and integrity. Let them know that you will be showing this letter to other people that are in similar situations to them, and who may be skeptical of your services.

> ▶ *Reputation Builder…* ◀ **Any time you help someone stay in their home, you become their hero and a friend for life. They will let everyone know what you did, how you helped them, and what a great guy or gal you are.**

This will also create additional business for you. You can use that testimonial and other testimonials when you go to someone else's door, to prove that you are what you say you are, and will do what you say you are going to do.

To Get the Forms for This Book and A Free Bonus Gift visit
www.FormsForBook.com

# What to Say at the Home

A lot of times, you will either call a pre-foreclosure or go to the door, and the people will tell you that they are all set and they've worked it out with the bank. Then a couple months later, you see the house going up for auction and you wonder what happened.

What happened was the homeowners were either in denial, or too embarrassed to ask for help. They assumed that everything was going to turn out all right, right up to the day of the foreclosure. Like a genie was going to come out of a bottle and, "Poof!" this nasty foreclosure business was going to disappear.

Since these people are in denial or are too embarrassed to ask for help, put together a package with your credentials and what you can do to help. Some things that may go into the package are a resume about who you are, and a copy of a Better Business Bureau letter stating that you are a member in good standing. Include letters from other organizations that you are a member of; letters from your banker; insurance agent; real estate broker; a member of the clergy; and anyone else who will say that you are an honest and fair person.

## The Most Important Part of Your Package

Most importantly, you want to put in **testimonial letters from people**, in situations just like theirs that you have already helped. **As many as you can get.** If you are just starting out and don't have any, use all of the letters mentioned above, and start collecting them.

> ▶ *Get and Use Testimonials!* ◀ **Testimonials are the most powerful tool you can use to entice someone to use your services. People will believe 10 times more what other people say about you than what you say about yourself.**

To Get the Forms for This Book and A Free Bonus Gift visit
www.FormsForBook.com

Get as many as you can, and keep on getting them. Testimonials are the most powerful tool you can use to entice someone to use your services. People will believe 10 times more what other people say about you than what you say about yourself. Sometimes they don't believe at all what you say about yourself, especially if they have never met you. Get testimonials and use them!

Leave that package with them and don't be surprised when you get a phone call a week or two later. Though don't wait for them to call. You should also be following up on a regular basis.

The deadline is set. They need to find a solution to the problem. If you are the one in front of them when they make that final decision to do something, you will get the business. Either follow up in person, by phone or by mail at least once a week, until the house is either sold, the back payments are made, or it goes up for foreclosure.

## Direct Mail and Pre-Foreclosures

The last method of contact is through direct mail. Look in the direct mail section of this manual for an in-depth analysis of how to write a good direct mail piece. A good direct mail piece will have AIDA. It will give the reader a compelling reason to pick up the phone to do business with you.

Always send your letters in a handwritten envelope (blue ink) with a live stamp. Do not put a company name in the return address area. **Do** put an address there. Whether or not you want to put your name is up to you.

You must have a headline on your letter. It must stand out and give the number one reason to do business with you. As you write the copy, you must create desire and finally a call-to-action, to get them to call you now.

Always put a P.S. on your letter. The P.S. should also restate the number one reason for doing business with you. The reason for this is after the person receiving the letter reads the headline; the next place they will look is to see who sent it. The P.S. will be right below your name, and the person will read this next.

Always, always, always use testimonials. Either make up a page of quotes that people have given you, or put in copies of actual letters that you have received. Always get permission from the person to use their testimonial in writing, and use their full name. If you do not use names on your testimonials, people will not believe that they are real.

There are examples of some good direct mail pieces on the following pages. Notice how they are laid out, and the message that is being conveyed. Use these (they work!), and take time to develop some of your own.

Good direct mail pieces will have people calling you to do business, instead of you making cold calls to get business. It's much easier to do business with someone who is already pre-sold on your services, than it is to try to convert someone who has no idea who you are.

You will notice that two of these letters use a two-step marketing campaign. The two-step campaign is explained in Chapter 10, Radio Ads. You can use the same special report that is included in that chapter, though you will need to change the cover page to match the title of the free report that is referred to in the letters at the end of this chapter.

## How Many Letters Should I Send?

Don't stop with the first letter. If they do not call you, follow up with a second, third, fourth, fifth and however many it takes until you get to the foreclosure date. Keep following up. Many people will not call you until after the third letter. Many investors stop sending letters after the second letter. There are a lot of people just looking for someone to help them out of their situation.

To Get the Forms for This Book and A Free Bonus Gift visit
www.FormsForBook.com

# Killer Negotiating Tips

Here is some advice when you begin to structure the deal to buy the property. If you are going to buy the house outright and not through an agreement for deed, let the people know that you are trying to create a win/win situation.

Your plan is to purchase the property, and by doing this you will stop the foreclosure process and thus save their credit. A foreclosure stays on their credit report for seven years.

So, instead of them losing the house to the bank, and all of their equity along with it, they will walk away with cash at the closing and they will able to begin again with a clean slate.

In return for closing quickly, you need to obtain the house for a certain price in order for you to make a profit. As an investor, you explain to them that you need to make a profit to stay in business. They will understand this. Show them what a fair profit is (at least $20,000). Add that to all of your other expenses that you will have with this deal, and deduct that from the After Repaired market Value (I use the Offer Calculation Worksheet that is in my "How To Estimate And Renovate Houses For Huge Profits Manual"; it is extremely effective.). Show them what the figures are, and 9 times out of 10, they will agree with you.

If they ask you for more for the house, explain to them that if you gave them more, you would not be able to stay in business. Remember, you are negotiating from a position of strength and they are negotiating from a position of weakness. That foreclosure date is looming!

# How to Obtain the Property Using "Agreement For Deed"

If you are doing an agreement for deed, you should give them the above benefits and offer them an amount of money that will be enough to get them out of the house and into their next living quarters, which will probably be an apartment.

To Get the Forms for This Book and A Free Bonus Gift visit
www.FormsForBook.com

This amount is usually around $5,000. You can give less and sometimes nothing. Of course, you should start negotiating at a lower amount. If they have a lot of equity in the house, you may offer them more. If so, structure the deal so that they do not receive the additional money until <u>after you resell the property</u>. This lowers the amount that you will have to come out of your pocket.

## The Hidden Benefit of "Agreement For Deed"

Also let them know that you will be making up their back payments (you will have to, to keep them out of foreclosure), and that this will keep them out of foreclosure, but you will also be making their monthly payments--on time--while you own the property. This will help re-establish their credit rating. Another benefit for them.

One time I made up 12 payments for a woman and took over her deed. I told her that I was going to lease option it and when the person was ready to buy, the mortgage would be paid off and taken out of her name.

After a year and a half of making the payments on time, she called me to tell me that she now had great credit and she was going to buy another house. I congratulated her. She told me that she wanted her name off of that mortgage because now she didn't want to risk her good credit rating. After I had made all those payments to re-establish her credit!! You can't please them all.

There are many ways to structure the deal. These are just a couple of them.

The thing to remember with pre-foreclosures is follow up, follow up, follow up, and use testimonials. Do these two things, and you will be very successful in this market.

## What If the House Goes to Auction?

If a property does go all the way to auction, here are a few simple strategies to help you become successful.

To Get the Forms for This Book and A Free Bonus Gift visit
www.FormsForBook.com

Go to other auctions first that you do not plan on bidding on. This will give you a feel for how an auction works, and you can start to develop strategies. Notice that there are a few people in the crowd that do not start bidding until the very end, when bidding becomes very slow and the bid increments become small. These are the experienced investors.

Always call the auctioneer the morning of the auction to check to make sure that the auction is still going to be taking place. A lot of times, auctions are cancelled or postponed because the homeowner filed for bankruptcy.

At every auction you will need to bring a certified bank check for a pre-specified amount of money, usually about $5,000. This money will be used as your deposit if you are the winning bidder. If you win, and do not go forward and buy the property, you will lose this money. Be sure that you want the property!

Always be pre-approved by a lending institution or hard-money lender before you get to the auction. You want to know exactly what you can afford, so that you don't bid out of your range. Most auctions allow you 30 days to complete the purchase. That's not a lot of time, so you want to have a head start in the process. Most of the time you can get an extension of you request it, but sometimes you can't; if you don't close, you will lose that $5,000 deposit.

Know what your maximum offer is going to be, <u>before</u> you start bidding. It's very easy to get caught up in the excitement and pay more than you really wanted for a property. Do not get emotionally attached to the property. Be ready to stop bidding as soon as it <u>gets $1 higher</u> than your preset high bid.

Dress as if you were the bank. At every auction, there is a representative from the lending institution that is foreclosing. Their job is to make sure that the bidding gets higher than what's owed on the property, or some other bottom-line price that the bank has pre-set.

If it looks as if the property is going to sell for less than the minimum pre-set price, then the bank steps in and starts bidding themselves. If no one bids as high as the bank, then the bank will buy back the property to protect its investment.

In most cases, the bank will at least bid as high as what is owed to them on the property. Sometimes at an auction you will see the bidding slow down at a certain figure.

Let's say for example purposes, the bidding starts to slow down at $81,000 and it looks like the property is going to sell. The bank may step in and give a bid of $134,219. That was the minimum price that the bank had to get, and since it looked like the bidding was going to stop well short of that mark, the bank stepped in and increased the bidding to that amount.

If the bidding slowed down at $125,000, you would see the bank start bidding up the price slowly. Many times they get above their minimum using this procedure.

## Dress Like the Banker

The trick is to dress like a banker and stand close to the auctioneer. Many experienced bidders will assume that you are the bank's bidder. Do not start bidding until the very end, when the bidding starts to get very slow. Someone who thought they were close to winning a bid and now see that you (the bank) are bidding, may get discouraged and drop out.

If you start to go to a lot of auctions, you will only be able to use this trick a few times because you'll notice that you will start to see the same faces there. People will begin to recognize you as another investor.

I learned this trick unwittingly. I went to one of my first auctions and I thought I was supposed to look successful, as if I could actually buy the property. So I wore a nice two-piece suit. I had done my homework and had set my maximum bid price at $151,000.

The bidding started at $100,000 and started up slowly until it reached $120,000. For some reason, the auctioneer jumped the bidding up from $120,000 to $130,000. A $10,000 increment when the bid increments had been $1,000. The last bid given was for $120,000, and now he was asking $130,000.

To Get the Forms for This Book and A Free Bonus Gift visit
www.FormsForBook.com

He said, "Who can give me 130, 130, who can give me 130. No one at 130? No one at 130? 120 going once, no one can give me 130? 120 going twice." At this point I thought that the property was just about to be sold at $120,000. Thirty one thousand lower than I had planned on spending.

I raised my hand and said 130. Nobody bid higher than me, and I got the property.

A funny thing happened after the bidding stopped. Three or four investors came over to me after the bidding to give me their card. They asked me to contact them when I was ready to sell the property. At first I was confused until I told the second guy that I was not going to resell it; I was going live in it and move my business here. The property had a four-car garage with offices up above.

"Move my business here? Aren't you from the bank?" he asked.

"No", I replied, "I'm from the next town over." After the fourth person tried to give me his card, I realized that every thought I was the bank and when I stepped in to start bidding, that's when everyone stopped.

I did this successfully a couple more times until I become known in the investment circles. Does it work all the time? No. Should you try it to see if it might work for you? Sure! What's the worst thing that could happen? Besides, you could get a great deal on a house!

You can get an idea of how much the bank is owed on the property by going to the registry of deeds and looking at the mortgages that have been filed on the property.

This will give you an idea of how much equity is in the property, and if there is a good chance that you will be able to buy the property at the auction. There is no sense wasting your time if the people owe close to what it is worth. The bank usually buys them back.

# Make Sure You Know Who is Foreclosing

Make sure you know who is foreclosing on the property. Is it a first mortgage foreclosure or a second mortgage foreclosure?

If it is a second mortgage foreclosure and you are the winning bidder, you will have to pay off the first mortgage before you sell the house.

If it is a first mortgage foreclosure then the only other thing that will have to be paid off are municipal liens and federal liens. You can check at the city or town hall to see what is owned the municipality, and the federal liens will be recorded at the registry of deeds. This is called doing your "due diligence".

Another thing to consider is if there is a tenant in the house, from the soon-to-be previous owner. If there is, and you buy the house at the auction, you are also buying the tenant. You will have to evict the tenant yourself. This could take months, so you should have some reserve money to make the mortgage payments while you are getting them out, and then doing any renovation work that may be needed.

Also, there is no guarantee that they will not trash the place before they leave. Make sure you account for a worst-case scenario when you figure out your highest bid.

If a there is a tenant in the property, you may not be able to get inside to take a look before you start to bid. This is very common. You can get a good indication of what the inside will look like, by looking at the outside.

These are just a few tips on how to work foreclosures. You should have some experience before you start doing auctions. There are a lot of drawbacks that you need to be aware of to be successful. Once you do have the experience, auctions are a great way to make money in the real estate investing game.

Both auctions and pre-foreclosures are a great way to make money. Of the two, pre-foreclosures can make you more money faster, because

To Get the Forms for This Book and A Free Bonus Gift visit
www.FormsForBook.com

you're dealing with very motivated sellers, and because they are present in all real estate markets. Pre-foreclosures should be one of the tools you use to become wealthy investing in real estate.

> ▶ *Preforeclosure Profits...* ◀ Both auctions and pre-foreclosures are a great way to make money. Of the two, pre-foreclosures can make you more money faster, because you're dealing with very motivated sellers, and because they are present in all real estate markets. Pre-foreclosures should be one of the tools you use to become wealthy investing in real estate.

# Income/Expense Sheet

Name  _____

Address  _____

Income:

Clients Income  _____ yearly

Spousal Income  _____ yearly

Other Income  _____ yearly

**Total Income**  _____

divided by 12 to get **total monthly income**  _____

**Debt:**

|  | Name | Monthly Payment |
|---|---|---|
| Credit Cards | _____ | _____ |
|  | _____ | _____ |
|  | _____ | _____ |
|  | _____ | _____ |
|  | _____ | _____ |
| Auto Loans | _____ | _____ |
|  | _____ | _____ |
| Other Debt | _____ | _____ |
|  | _____ | _____ |

**Total Debt**  _____

**Other Outflow:**

| | |
|---|---|
| Food | _____ |
| Heat | _____ |
| Electricity | _____ |
| Gas (Auto) | _____ |
| Insurance (Auto) | _____ |
| Insurance (Health) | _____ |
| Cable TV | _____ |
| Internet | _____ |
| Kids Cloths | _____ |
| Kids Supplies | _____ |
| Kids Activities | _____ |

**Total Outflow**  _____

**Total Income**  _____

**Surplus/Deficit**  _____

# How To Stop Your Financial Problems
## In Seven Days or Less!

Dear Denise,

Would you be interested in a **free** consumer's report that has helped many other homeowners out of financial problems in five days or less?

Many people find themselves in financial problems, often through no fault of their own. It seems to happen overnight. One day everything is fine and life is good, and then the next day the phone doesn't stop ringing from bill collecting wolves hounding you for money that you don't have!

The **free** consumer's report, "How to Stop Your Financial Problems in Seven Days or Less," will show you how to stop that phone from ringing and allow you to once again take control of your own destiny.

This report is for anyone who wants to know:

- ✓ How to avoid a bank foreclosure
- ✓ How to find help to make up back mortgage payments
- ✓ How to sell a home quickly and profitably
- ✓ How to clean up a credit report
- ✓ How to file for bankruptcy without paying outrageous legal fees
- ✓ Free financial counseling

To have your **free** consumer's report, "How to Stop Your Financial Problems in Seven Days or Less," call our 24-hour, pre-recorded toll-free telephone number at 1-800-894-xxxx ext 4422. Simply leave your name and address, and we will send the report to you immediately. Supplies are limited, so call now!

Before you speak to anyone regarding current financial problems, order this report. It will save you time and money! Call now!

Sincerely,


David Lindahl
Financial Specialist

P.S. Problems are solved with information and education. Order your **free** copy of the consumer report, " How to Solve Your Financial Problems In Seven Days or Less," and learn how to solve your financial problems now!

## Who Else Wants <u>FREE</u> Advice To
## Solve Their Financial Problems?

Dear Homeowner,

**W**ould you be interested in a **free** consumer's report that has helped many other homeowners out of their financial problems?

Many people find themselves in financial problems, often through no fault of their own. It seems to happen overnight. One day everything is fine and life is good, and then the next day the phone doesn't stop ringing from bill collecting wolves, hounding you for money that you don't have!

The **free** consumer's report, "Seven Proven Steps To Solve Your Financial Problems" will show you how to stop that phone from ringing and allow you to once again take control of your life.

This report is for anyone who wants to know:

    ✓  How to avoid a bank foreclosure
    ✓  How to find help to make up back mortgage payments
    ✓  How to sell a home quickly and profitably
    ✓  How to clean up a credit report
    ✓  How to file for bankruptcy without paying outrageous legal fees
    ✓  Free financial counseling

To have your **free** consumer's report, "Seven Proven Steps To Solve Your Financial Problems," call our 24-hour, pre-recorded toll-free telephone number at 1-800-894-xxxx ext 4422. Simply leave your name and address, and we will send the report to you immediately. Supplies are limited, so call now!

If you would like to speak to me directly, call me at 617-835-xxxx and I can begin counseling you over the phone. This is a **free** service.

Before you speak to anyone regarding current financial problems, order this report.  It will save you time and money! Call now!

                            Sincerely,

                            David Lindahl
                            Financial Specialist

P.S. Problems are solved with information and education.  Order your **free** copy of the consumer report, " Seven Proven Steps To Solve Your Financial Problems," and learn how to solve your financial problems now!

To Get the Forms for This Book and A Free Bonus Gift visit
www.FormsForBook.com

# Stop Your Upcoming Foreclosure In Nine Days Or Less...
## Don't Let the Bank Take Your Property!

Name
Address
City, State

Dear Friend,

You can stop your foreclosure in nine days or less by selling your house for **CASH,** using a program that can possibly create equity.

We will pay you cash for your house at fair market value, not a distressed foreclosure price. If you do nothing, hoping for a miracle, the law will sell your house at Public Auction, meaning your house could be sold for 25 to 50 percent below value. Don't allow this to happen!

This is a money solution that will allow you to rebuild your future, but you must act now. **Time is your worst enemy: Don't be embarrassed or humiliated by a lender who cares nothing about your problems.**

We've been in a similar situation as yours, yet at that time, nobody lent us a helping hand. We want to provide you with that helping hand by supplying you with **KNOWLEDGE, CASH, AND OUR ABILITY TO KEEP YOUR CREDITORS FROM ANNOYING YOU!**

### What Will We Do When You Call Us At 1-800-478-xxxx?

➢ David or Tammy will answer the phone and ask you several questions about your home, in order to start an evaluation.
➢ We will set up a time to visit you at your home, to discuss our proposal. Our services are **FREE**. You incur **no** cost. Not everyone qualifies for our program, but we are very flexible.
➢ We can communicate with your lender. They will deal directly with us, because we have the cash to handle past-due payments.

This can be done in one visit, but you must call us to begin this process. **Ask for David or Tammy at 1-800-478-xxxx day or night.** If we are out, leave us a message.

To Get the Forms for This Book and A Free Bonus Gift visit
www.FormsForBook.com

### You Can Walk Away Free and Clear
### With Cash and a Fresh Start

We feel that most people may be skeptical for one major reason: They have been given empty promises in the past. This is why we offer a written guarantee:

*Please turn to next page…*
**********************************************************
******************************************

# Our Guarantee To You:

*If You Receive a Written Offer That is More Beneficial Than Our Proposal,*
*We Will Cancel Our Agreement,*
*Regardless of How Far Along We Are in the Process*

**********************************************************
************
..................................................................

**So you be the judge. If you call us you can't lose. If you do not, your indecision may cost you thousands of dollars; your**

**property is sold at auction.**

Make this a **TURNING POINT** in your life. **Just reach for the phone and dial 1-800-478-xxxx, toll free. Ask for Tammy or David. We can help!!**

With kindest regards,

David Lindahl

P.S. When you call us, rest assured that you will be under no obligation-- and you can have your foreclosure problem solved in nine days or less!

To Get the Forms for This Book and A Free Bonus Gift visit
www.FormsForBook.com

# They Were Skeptical When I Told Them That I Could
# Stop Their Foreclosure In Nine Days Or Less... But They Were All Smiles When It Actually Happened!

Name
Address
State Zip

Dear Name,

Don't lose hope..help is on the way! Our company has helped other homeowners in foreclosure to regain financial stability and self respect by stopping the foreclosure process IN NINE DAYS OR LESS.

We can offer you an alternative or "fresh start" from a dismal situation, by purchasing the equity in your house and releasing you from the burden brought about by the foreclosure process.

Although it seems that life is not always fair (it's not!), you can escape from this negative situation by using one of the many programs that we have to offer. By offering such programs, **we only benefit when you do.**

### Our Company Can Offer You Several Benefits:

➢ CASH – Instead of losing your home to the bank and being left with nothing, we will buy your home and give you **CASH** to make a fresh start.
➢ Because we will prevent you from going into foreclosure, a foreclosure will not be recorded on your credit report (foreclosures are on reports for seven years!).
➢ Moving expenses can be paid by us.
➢ Our ability to communicate directly with your lender should eliminate annoying phone calls and angry letters.

To Get the Forms for This Book and A Free Bonus Gift visit
www.FormsForBook.com

> We may be able to provide temporary housing and in some cases six months of no rental payments.

You may be wondering to yourself, "Do offers such as these actually exist?" **They do!** That is why I have attached a couple of letters from people whom we have been able to help in the past. We are also a member of the Better Business Bureau. Give them a call. They will tell you that we are a reputable company that has been helping people in situations such as yours for a number of years.

## *We Will Offer You CASH*

We are in the business of providing **CASH SOLUTIONS**. We provide knowledge of how the system works beneficially for you as well as us. We work only for "Win/Win" situations. You must receive benefits for us to be able to make a deal.  We also offer you the following guarantee:
\*\*\*\*\*\*\*\*\*\*\*\*\*\*\*\*\*\*\*\*\*\*\*\*\*\*\*\*\*\*\*\*\*\*\*\*\*\*\*\*\*\*\*\*\*\*\*\*\*\*\*\*\*\*\*\*\*\*\*\*\*\*\*\*

### Our Guarantee to You:
*If you receive a written offer that is more beneficial than our proposal, we will cancel our agreement, no matter how far along we are in the process.*
\*\*\*\*\*\*\*\*\*\*\*\*\*\*\*\*\*\*\*\*\*\*\*\*\*\*\*\*\*\*\*\*\*\*\*\*\*\*\*\*\*\*\*\*\*\*\*\*\*\*\*\*\*\*\*\*\*\*\*\*\*\*\*\*

You can't turn back time, but you can change your immediate situation by allowing us to purchase your home for cash in nine days or less, so you can walk away from this burden forever!

Remember, you must forget the past. **It's time to focus on solutions, not problems**.
We look forward to providing you with the **CASH** you need to get on with your life.
Pick up the phone and call **NOW**. Even the phone call is free! 1-800-478-xxx

With kindest regards,

**David Lindahl**
Results Home Buyers, Inc.

P.S. Think of the peace of mind you will have when we stop your current foreclosure!

To Get the Forms for This Book and A Free Bonus Gift visit
www.FormsForBook.com

Here are some sample testimonials that I have gotten, and this is how I add them to my direct mail letters. I always use a different color paper when I add them to my mailings. I usually use a light yellow. This is the layout I use. I always put the person's last name and town. You will want to do that, too. I left them out here because this is a home study course and I need get permission to use my client's names.

**Here Are Comments From People That Were In The Exact Same Position You Are In... People Just Like You...**

"Thank you so much for coming to the rescue and allowing us to move forward with our lives. Your ability to take over when all other options failed us was truly 'what the doctor ordered.'"

*John H., East Boston*

"I am grateful to you, Dave, not only for your valuable assistance, but also for your tenacity in convincing me that your program was not a 'scam.' I'll admit that it seemed too good to be true, and therefore I was a little (O.K. maybe a lot!) skeptical at first, but I am convinced that no solution would have been found for me through what most people consider to be conventional channels."

*Ernst S., Easton*

"Not only did you find us a way to make up the back payments, you did everything you said you were going to do. Thank you for your honesty."

*Gladys V., Malden*

"…I thought I was going to lose the house to the bank and I was going to be branded with a foreclosure on my credit report for the next seven years…Instead of losing everything, you saved my credit rating and I put money in my bank account!!"

*Nicole D., Brockton*

# Chapter 4

## Chunkers

If you listen to a lot of gurus, they tell you that the way to make money in the real estate business is through "pretty houses". While you can make a great deal of money using that method, one of the biggest problems that you will face is that your equity is tied up until the option is exercised sometime down the road. The other problem is that, although you have a positive cash flow, it's usually somewhere between $200 to $400, you're going to have to do a lot of pretty houses in the beginning before you make some real headway.

When I first started out with my partner, we bought a three-family house using credit cards for the down payment. I had read somewhere to get as many credit cards as possible (cards that would not charge you an annual fee), and get the credit line as high as you could qualify for so that you can use these cards for down payments and for purchasing houses.

Well, we bought our first three multi-family houses this way. They were all rehab projects. We bought them cheap, rehabbed them and then refinanced to get our money back to pay off the credit cards.

It took a long time to rehab those three family houses. While we were doing those rehabs and waiting to refinance, other good deals were popping up. We were able to buy two more multi-family homes before we ran out of credit card money.

So, we did the only logical thing for us at the time, and that was to buy "chunkers." You see, our main concern was how we were going to get our next deposit for the multi-family deals that were out there. Prices in our area were outrageously low. They were so low that the *Boston Herald* had an ad in the real estate section that read, "Brockton three family, buy one get one free $25,000!" We wanted to get as many multi-family properties under our control as possible, and our plan was to eventually live off of the positive cash flow as our economy got better. I had read

To Get the Forms for This Book and A Free Bonus Gift visit
www.FormsForBook.com

about doing this in one of the many real estate investing books and tapes that I read and listened to, and it sounded like a good idea. It was.

So we started buying single-family houses, fixing them up and then flipping them for a minimum of a $20,000 profit. In the beginning, while we were getting our act together, a couple of houses came in at less than $20,000, but $20,000 was our goal and more often than not we either hit it or exceeded it.

We would then take this chunk of money and use it to buy more multi-family properties. Hence the word "chunker" entered our vocabulary. We love "chunkers." Loved them then and love them even more today.

## How I got a $42,000 "chunk" in less than nine days.

A "chunker" doesn't always need to be a complete rehab either. Early this year I met with a woman who had her house on the market for $129,900. She called the "We Buy Houses" sign that I have on my work truck and told me that she just fired her realtor and she needed to sell her house to get to Alabama.

I said, "Ma'am, I'll be right over!"

I got there and it turned out that the realtor had had the house under agreement two times but couldn't get it to the closing. Frustrated, the owner fired her, called me and told me that she would sell it to me for $80,000 if I could close by the end of the month.

The house itself was not in a great neighborhood and abutted a parking lot for old box trucks on one side, and had a loading dock and an ice house across the street (this building ran up the entire block). The house was in O.K. shape, maybe in need of a new kitchen floor, repair of some wallpaper, paint and some nice landscaping out front to pretty it up and separate it from its surroundings.

To Get the Forms for This Book and A Free Bonus Gift visit
www.FormsForBook.com

In that market it was worth $129,900. I told her I would be able to pay her $75,000 for the house and could close quickly. She said that she would have to sit down and calculate exactly what she was going to need. She looked up at me and said that $78,000 was her bottom line.

Now this woman was motivated! She gave me all I needed to know during our interview. She wanted to be in Alabama! She wanted to be in Alabama yesterday! She also let slip that part of the money she was looking for was to pay off her car and get a new one. Certainly not a necessity!

So I countered her $78,000 counter offer and said, "Ma'am, at $75,000 I will have you packed and on your way to Alabama in three days." Just as I thought, she said the new car could wait and away she went -- very, very happy!

I could have jumped on the $80,000 price for the house and still made a better than average profit, but the reason I negotiated down was because of past experiences.

## Two Quick Money Making Rules Of Negotiating

From past experience, I've learned a couple of rules of negotiating. Number one, he who states a price first loses. Number two, I have had deals in the past go bad because I accepted the first offer that the seller made to me (because it was reasonable), and then a few days went by and they started thinking that they should have asked for more for the house because I accepted the first offer. In this scenario, usually then all kinds of weird things start happening.

Like the seller decides not to sell, or the seller decides that two weeks into the deal that it is time to negotiate for more money, or (even worse) they sign a contract with someone else for more money without telling you and then call and cancel the deal. Even though you are already under contract!

So no matter how low a seller goes with an initial price, I always try to negotiate it lower. This eliminates what I call seller's remorse.

To Get the Forms for This Book and A Free Bonus Gift visit
www.FormsForBook.com

So I negotiated less on this house and sold it for $124,900 eight days later, as is. That was a $42,000 "chunk" after I paid the realtor commission and attorney fees.

This deal worked because the owner was motivated, and after talking to the original realtor who had had it under agreement twice, I found out that her son was living in the basement and didn't want to move so he would not let any home inspectors in to inspect the property, which is why she couldn't close the deal.

I happened to be on the scene when the son was away on a trip. Another reason the seller was motivated! She wanted to be out of town before he came back, and she was. He came home and there was a sold sign out front and the locks were changed. Mama was in Alabama, spending her proceeds!

## How "Chunking" Can Make You Very Wealthy

There are many ways to become wealthy in real estate.

The way that I used was to buy multi-family residential properties and hold them long term. This creates a reliable passive monthly income and lets your tenants pay off your mortgage, thus creating more equity and wealth for yourself.

I use "chunkers" to give me the down payments so that I can buy more multi-families. My minimum profit per deal is $20,000. With this $20,000, I look for a multi-family property that is in need of repairs, is mismanaged, or one where the rents are low so that I have some built-in equity.

You can get some great deals from people who have entered the landlord game without educating themselves on how to play properly. They tend to burn out fast, and you do them a great service by taking over their property!

Being a landlord isn't hard, but you must educate yourself. You can get books and tapes, join a property owners association, and even

To Get the Forms for This Book and A Free Bonus Gift visit
www.FormsForBook.com

attend classes at the Institute of Real Estate Management, which holds classes throughout the country at different times of the year. However you attain your knowledge is up to you, but you **must** attain it or you will join the many other former burnt out landlords who sold their gold mine properties to shrewd investors like myself, someone who takes the time to continually educate himself.

The one thing you must learn is how to control your tenants so that your tenants are not controlling you. This is the number one reason that landlords lose money!

So we purchase the property, fix whatever problems that it may have and raise the rents accordingly. We started out buying three- to six-unit buildings. We are now buying 20- to 40-unit complexes. We won't stop until we get our own complexes over 100 units each.

Sure, this method may take you a little longer to be able to quit your job, because you will be reinvesting your profits. But if you work a little harder in the beginning, you will become much wealthier in the end.

Basically, what we do is attract and seek out motivated sellers of single-family houses and multi-family buildings. We use the single-family rehabs to give us a "chunk" of money so that we can invest in multi-family housing. We use the multi-family properties to give us passive monthly income and create greater wealth through equity creation (tenants paying our mortgages).

You can use "chunkers" in a variety of other ways to become wealthy as well. You can just keep reinvesting in more "chunkers" and throwing the left over "chunks" of money in your savings or IRA accounts and watch that money grow (and it will grow and grow and grow). Soon you'll be financing your own rehab deals and won't have to pay hard money lender fees (hard money lenders loan money to real estate investors at high interest rates) and eventually you will have so much excess cash in your accounts you can become a hard money lender yourself. As all this starts happening for you, it won't be long before you become a "chunker" junkie!

To Get the Forms for This Book and A Free Bonus Gift visit
www.FormsForBook.com

# *Chapter 5*
# **Marketing**

### Getting The Deals

There are many different ways to get deals;
>Flyers
>Direct Mail
>Internet
>Foreclosures
>Attorneys
>Ant Farms
>Bird Dogs
>Real Estate Agents
>Signs
>Business Cards
>Classifieds
>Ant Farms

In this Chapter, I'm going to cover two of the most common ways to get deals, Direct Mail and Real Estate Brokers.

That's not to say that you should only be doing two types of marketing. I believe in doing at least 5 – 7 different types of marketing so deals continuously trickle into you pipeline.

That being said, let's get you started with these two!

Picture this: You're sitting in your home, the phone rings, and it's a motivated seller looking to sell their property. An hour later the phone rings again. It's another motivated seller also looking to get out of their property. During the day, you have had a total of eight phone calls from people who are interested in selling their property.

What is going on? Why are you getting so many calls in one day when you have spent previous months searching for deals and didn't have any luck? These people are responding to your direct mail campaign. You've sent them a letter (and gave them a compelling reason to call you), and now they are doing just that.

> ▶ *Direct Mail Delivers...* ◀ **Not only is direct mail a great way to get leads, but these are the easiest people to do business with. They have already pre-qualified themselves by calling you, and they are certainly motivated.**

This is the beauty of direct mail. Having your target customers raise their hand by calling you and telling you that they want to do business with you. Not only is this a great way to get leads, but these are the easiest people to do business with. They have already pre-qualified themselves by calling you, and they are certainly motivated.

## Three Components of a Direct Mail Campaign

The basic components of a direct mail campaign include targeting a list of people to mail to, creating a message to fit that target, and giving them a compelling reason to call you.

Direct mail is a numbers game. If you receive a one to two percent response from your mailing, that's good. That's what you should expect. That means for every 1,000 pieces that you mail out, you should receive responses from five to 10 people.

It doesn't sound like a lot, but if you can purchase just one house from that mailing at an average profit of $20,000, you will more than make your money back.

I once sent 1,000 letters to out-of-state owners of multi-family buildings and only got three people to respond. Fortunately, one of those three was a gentleman from Florida who was tired of being a long distance landlord. He told me that he wanted to sell his three-family property for the assessed value only that it needed some work, and he wanted to sell it "as is".

He told me that from talking to some friends that lived in the area, if he did the work to the property and fixed it up, they said he could get a lot more, but he'd had enough and wanted out.

So I bought it for the assessed value, painted the exterior ($3,500), took down old wallpaper and repainted the units ($4,100), refinished the floors ($1,400) and added some linoleum in the kitchens and baths ($2,000. Total rehab: $11,000). The property is now worth $130,000 more that what I paid for it! You don't have to find too many of those to make you happy!

## Two Types of Direct Mail Campaigns

There are two different approaches to a direct mail campaign. The first is to plan a series of two or three mailings to the same group or list. These mailing are called steps. If you plan to send three consecutive mailings (which should be about seven days apart), this is called a three-step mailing campaign.

These campaigns are designed to get the target to raise their hand and call you to do business directly, or you could offer a Free Special Report that will entice the person to raise their hand for the report and will identify the person as a means of future business.

When starting a direct mail campaign, the first thing you want to do is to select your target market. You want to answer the question, "What group or groups of people would most likely respond to my offer?"

Below is a list of groups of people that, for some reason or another, would probably contain a better-than-average amount of motivated sellers:

- Pre-Foreclosures – people at the start of the foreclosure process
- Expired Listings

To Get the Forms for This Book and A Free Bonus Gift visit
www.FormsForBook.com

- Out-of-Town Owners
- Landlords Evicting Tenants
- Property Owners Going To Court For Health Violations
- People Getting a Divorce
- Attorneys – Estate and Divorce Attorneys
- Obituaries

You will find lists of these people in the following places:

- ✓ Pre-Foreclosures – Local and financial newspaper, court house, list service providers
- ✓ Expired Listings – Multiple listing service, realtor relationships
- ✓ Out of Town Owners – Town or City Assessor's Office
- ✓ Landlords Evicting Tenants – Housing Court
- ✓ Property Owners With Health Violations – Housing Court, local board of health officials (ask them which landlords may be in trouble)
- ✓ People Getting A Divorce – Probate Court
- ✓ Attorneys – Telephone book
- ✓ Obituaries – Local newspapers

A direct mail campaign can be done with either letters or postcards. Postcards work well because you don't have to worry about the prospect opening the letter. A lot of people sort their mail over the wastebasket, and throw away anything that remotely looks like junk mail.

With a postcard, you can capture the prospect's attention with a compelling headline and create interest that will compel them to read the rest of the text.

The drawback of postcards is that you're working with limited space to tell your story and get your prospect to act.

When sending a letter, on the other hand, it can be as many pages as you think necessary to get the prospect to call you.

To Get the Forms for This Book and A Free Bonus Gift visit
www.FormsForBook.com

Some people may think, "Who would read a long sales letter? I certainly wouldn't." The person who reads a long sales letter would be someone who truly needed your services. There is an adage in the direct marketing business: "The more you tell, the more you sell."

The first thing you need to do with a letter is **get the thing opened.** You must slip below the prospect's radar screen that is zoned in on detecting junk mail as they sort through the mail over the trash barrel.

# The Right Way to Address an Envelope for Big Response

You do this by using plain number 10 envelopes, hand addressing every envelope with blue pen, putting your name and return address in the upper left hand corner, and using a live stamp.

If you really want to get below their radar, you could use a square envelope, though this can become costly. The receiver may think that they are getting an invitation, which they actually are…an invitation to purchase your product or service. They may be more inclined to open the envelope.

## *The Wrong Way to Address an Envelope*

Here are some don'ts for envelopes, any one of which will dramatically lower the amount of people who open your envelope:

> ➢ Don't use labels (O.K. for postcards)
> ➢ Don't use metered postage
> ➢ Don't put a business name in the upper-left-hand corner
> ➢ Don't computer generate the names and address on the envelope
> ➢ Don't use bulk rate (only 50 percent actually get delivered)

You should be delegating these menial tasks to someone else. The going rate to stamp, stuff and address an envelope is 11 cents per

To Get the Forms for This Book and A Free Bonus Gift visit
www.FormsForBook.com

envelope, and is well worth it. This frees you up to go find other deals. Not only that, but it gets done. If you leave it up to yourself, you may have a tendency to put it off. Remember, consistency is the key to marketing.

You should plan your mailing so that your target receives the postcard or letter on a Tuesday, Wednesday, or Thursday. Never on a Friday or Saturday, because people are too busy making plans for or enjoying the weekend. On Mondays they are trying to recuperate from the weekend, and are too busy making plans for the workweek.

Having your mail delivered on a Tuesday, Wednesday or Thursday will increase your response rate.

Now you've got your prospect to open the envelope or look at the postcard. They will take the **next two seconds** to decide whether or not they will read the rest of the text, or throw it in the trash.

You only have two seconds to grab their attention and give them a reason to read your message. You must have a bold, compelling headline that immediately answers the question, "What's in it for me?"

## How to Create a Compelling Headline

Your headline is the most important part of your direct mail piece. If your headline does not entice them to read further, it doesn't matter how good the rest of the material is…they will never see it!

Here are the elements for a great headline--what your headline must accomplish:
> Attract attention
> Stimulate curiosity and intrigue
> Reveal the strongest benefit of your offer
> Make news, or be seen as new or different
> Be specific and meaningful to your prospect

To Get the Forms for This Book and A Free Bonus Gift visit
www.FormsForBook.com

# Eight Ready-To-Use Compelling Headlines

Your headline should contain the primary benefit that the person will receive from doing business with you. For example:

✓ (Pre-Foreclosure :) Stop Your Foreclosure In Seven Days Or Less

✓ Expired Listing :) Who Else Wants To Sell Their House In Five Days Or Less?

✓ (Out of Town Owner :) Prices In Boston Have Never Been Higher, Now Is The Time To Sell. Don't Miss Out On This Incredible Market! Read On…

✓ (Landlords :) There Is Nothing Sweeter Than Selling An Investment Property That Has Become A Pain In The Ass

✓ (Health Violators :) Has Your Investment Property Become A Headache? I've Got The Cure…

✓ (Divorce :) Selling Soon? Highest Prices Paid For Your Real Estate

✓ (Attorneys :) A Reliable, Trusted Investment Company To Purchase Your Clients' Properties. Our Complaint-Free Record With The Better Business Bureau Makes You Look Good.

✓ (Obituaries :) We Buy Houses For Cash, Fast Closings

▶ *The Headline is Key!* ◀ **Your headline is the most important part of your direct mail piece. If your headline does not entice them to read further, it doesn't matter how good the rest of the material is…they will never see it!**

Can you see how these headlines are designed to grab the reader's attention and entice them to read further? If you were a frustrated owner whose listing had just expired, wouldn't you want to know how someone plans to sell your home in five days or less, when the real estate agent couldn't do it in 180 days?

If you were in pre-foreclosure and someone claimed that they could stop your foreclosure in seven days or less, don't you think that you would stand up and take notice?

This is why the headline is the most important part of any direct marketing piece. When using a postcard, repeat the headline on both sides. On the front, simply instruct the reader to turn the card over to learn more.

You should write a list of 10 to 20 headlines for each direct marketing piece that you send out. Go through the list and choose the most compelling, attention-grabbing, "I've got to have that!" headline, and use it.

If you are stuck writing your headlines, look through newspapers, magazines and on magazine covers to get ideas.

Here is a list of some famous headlines that, by simply changing a few words, I've been able to use in my investment business. The underlined words are the original headline. These headlines have been used for years, with great success, in almost every industry. They've been used this long because they work:

- ➤ "They Laughed When I Told Them That I Could Stop Their Foreclosure In Seven Days Or Less, But When The Bank Didn't Show Up For The Auction, They Couldn't Stop Thanking Me"

- ➤ "Which One Of These Costly Home Selling Mistakes Will You Make?"

- ➤ "Who Else Wants to sell their house in five days or less?"

- ➤ "How To Rid Yourself Of Ungrateful Tenants And Put A Chunk Of Cash In Your Pocket"
- ➤ "Here's Free Advice For Homeowners Who Want To Sell Their House Quickly"

To Get the Forms for This Book and A Free Bonus Gift visit
www.FormsForBook.com

Now simply use these headlines or change the words to benefit your situation.

Remember, headlines are designed to do one thing--get your reader to read the first sentence of your text.

Your first sentence is designed to do one thing-- get the reader to read the second sentence. So you want to open with a very powerful first sentence. A good method to follow is to describe the problem that they now face, and you need to **emotionally charge** your letter by reminding them of the pain that they are now in. Remember, you didn't cause the pain, but you do have the cure.

# The Two Reasons That People Will Do Business With You

Now it's time to craft your message (your offer). People will decide to do business with you for two reasons:

1) **You Can Provide The Solution To Their Problem;**
2) **They Get Benefits And Positive Feelings From Doing Business With You.**

You must focus on what people want, not what they need. People do not buy needs; they buy the satisfaction they get from their wants. To create a response from your target, you must address their strongest desires.

Most people want solutions--to make more money, have more leisure time or more conveniences, to make life easier, gain self confidence, to be successful, to be proud, respected, to be a master of their own destiny, and to hold influence over others.

Most people want to avoid looking foolish, losing money, taking risks that will jeopardize their current situation, pain (emotional or physical), and personal embarrassment.

To Get the Forms for This Book and A Free Bonus Gift visit
www.FormsForBook.com

The better you can craft your message using what people want and what they want to avoid, the more successful your direct mail campaign will be.

Fill your copy with what benefits your targets will receive from doing business with you. Let them know what you can do for them. Make an immense promise. Let them know that you can do something remarkable. The average person sees over 10,000 marketing messages a day; you need to separate yours from the pack. Hype it up! Make the benefits impossible to ignore.

Keep in mind that you must also be believable and credible. You do this by backing up your promise with proof, especially from people you have already helped. These are called testimonials. **They are the most powerful way to get total strangers to believe in you.**

People will believe what other people say about you, before they will believe what you say about yourself. Ask your past clients to write a letter saying what a great service you provided them, how you helped them out of a tough situation, and what a great person you are!

Collect these letters and either put a couple in your direct mail piece, or make a page of quotes to get your point across. When using testimonials, you will need to get written permission from your clients. Always use their name and town at the end of the testimonial. If you don't, people will not believe that they are true.

## How to Create a Strong Sense of Urgency

You will want to create a strong sense of urgency throughout your letter. Convey to the target that they must **act now** in order to benefit from your services. Portray the illusion of scarcity. One way to promote limited scarcity in real estate investing is to let them know that you have limited funds available, and you are looking at several deals. If you are offering free special reports, let them know that supplies are limited--first come, first serve.

Inform your target that you are a "specialist" in their situation. People like to do business with specialists. You could be a Foreclosure Specialist,

Real Estate Specialist, Multi-Family Specialist…be creative and specific to their situation.

Throughout the text of your letter, you want to remind the target of the pain that they are in. Some direct marketers call this "sticking in the knife and turning it slowly." For every element of pain that you introduce, you want to offer a practical, credible solution. The solution may be an offer for a free special report or some other mechanism you're offering to solve their problem.

You'll want to explain your solutions and detail the benefits of those solutions. You must tell people what and how you will accomplish your solutions for them. You must elaborate on how much easier your solutions will make their life, how much they will gain by using you, and how much better off they'll be by using you than they will be by not using you.

## How to Handle Objections Before They Arise

As you are writing your text, you want to think of any objections that the target may have to doing business with you, and address them in the text. This will also increase your response. You also want to reveal any flaws that you may have and turn them into a benefit, thus preventing your letter from appearing "too good to be true" and unbelievable.

Use examples of other people that you have helped to prove your point and increase your credibility. Try to get testimonials from these people and add them in as well. This is a powerful one-two punch.

As you are writing your text, you will want to warn the target of what will happen if they do not take action. You are in essence predicting the future, increasing the target's pain by showing them what will happen if they do not take action.

You will also want to explain that doing business with you is risk free. Explain to the target that you cannot help everyone, but by setting up a simple appointment and going over the facts, you can determine if you may be able to help them out of their situation. If you cannot, you may be able to refer them to someone who can. Let them know that there is no obligation, and that your services are free.

To Get the Forms for This Book and A Free Bonus Gift visit
www.FormsForBook.com

You are in essence taking the pressure off. This will at least get you into the door of a lot of prospective sellers' homes.

Right before you close your letter or postcard, you will need to remind the target of all the benefits that they will be getting.

There are many ways to do this. You can use a story of how you delivered benefits to someone else who was facing a similar problem. Come right out and tell them in a straight-forward statement; use a testimonial from another client who got the same benefits; or use bullet points of what benefits people receive from using your services.

## Add a Strong "Call to Action"

The very last element that you should put in your letter or postcard is a **call to action.** You want to explain to the target exactly what they need to do. This can be done in a simple sentence, for example, "To stop the foreclosure of your home, pick up the phone and call me now at 555-1212."

Adding this call to action will dramatically increase your response.

## The Post Script – The Second Most Important Part of Your Letter/Postcard

After you sign the letter, **you must put in a powerful P.S.** When a target opens a letter or looks at a postcard, the first thing they will do is read the headline. After their interest is piqued, they will want to know who sent the piece, so they will look down at the signature. When they look at the signature, they will be drawn to the P.S. and will read it.

Your P.S. should restate the problem, restate the most desirable benefit, and include another call to action. You may add other items such as a special bonus, a risk-free guarantee and/or an element of scarcity.

To Get the Forms for This Book and A Free Bonus Gift visit
www.FormsForBook.com

There you have it! All the ingredients of a successful direct marketing piece. After you've written a piece you'll want to test it. Remember, you are looking for a one to two percent response rate.

If after testing you do not get the response that you wanted, go back and check all of the elements of the letter to make sure you didn't leave anything out. When you go to make changes, it's important that you only change one thing at a time so you know which change was responsible for the change in response. If you test more that one thing at a time, you won't know what worked and what didn't. This knowledge will help you with every new direct marketing piece you do.

Direct marketing is the easiest way to get motivated sellers to call you. You should become a student of direct marketing, as it can make you very wealthy. Not only should you read additional books on the subject, but you should start reading and studying all that junk mail that you receive, especially if you get the same thing more than one time, because that means the piece is working for someone.

If you find something good, don't be afraid to change it to fit your business. This is how a lot of good direct marketing campaigns begin.

The following pages are direct mail pieces that I have created and used successfully. Put them in the mail today, and make some money with them!

# Selling Soon?
# Highest Prices Paid For Your Real Estate!

Jane and Joe Smith
123 Main St.
Any Town, USA

Dear Jane and Joe,

I'm a real estate investor looking to buy properties in your neighborhood. I'm contacting local homeowners in the hopes that you may be interested in selling your property to me.

I'm part of a group that buys between 5 and 10 houses per month and would like to buy your house next. I can either close quickly, or take as much time as you like.

This is what will happen when you call me: I'll come over and take a look at your house. Next I'll compare it to other similar houses that have recently sold in the area. I will then offer you a fair price to purchase your property.

It's that simple. No aggressive realtors to deal with, no "For Sale" sign in front of your house; and no parade of people coming through your house at all hours of the day, night and weekends, checking out all of your stuff, and asking you questions that are none of their business anyway.

To find out what I can offer you for your house, call me now at 555-5555. I look forward to our speaking.

Sincerely,

David Lindahl

P.S. – For a quick, quiet, confidential sale of your property, call me **now** at 555-5555.

To Get the Forms for This Book and A Free Bonus Gift visit
www.FormsForBook.com

# We Buy Houses
## Any Area, Any Condition
### *Fast Closings!*

*Name*

Address
City, State


Dear Name,

Are you or is anyone you know looking to sell a property quickly?

I'm a local investor looking to purchase real estate in your area. I am interested in any property, whether it is in need of a lot of repair or in "move-in" condition.

I'm willing to pay a fair market price and can close quickly or take as long as you want.

How does this work? Simply call me at 555 –5555, I'll come out and take a look at the property. I'll compare it to similar properties that have sold in the area, and make you an offer.

As I stated before, I have the ability to pay cash and close quickly. For a **free** evaluation of your property, or if you want to tell me about somebody else's property (I'll give you a cash bonus if I buy it!), call me know at 555-5555.

I look forward to our speaking.

Kindest regards,

David Lindahl

P.S. For a fast closing and a fair price for your property (or someone's whom you know), call me now at 555-5555.


To Get the Forms for This Book and A Free Bonus Gift visit
www.FormsForBook.com

**Finally A Reliable, Trusted Investment Company To Purchase Your Clients' Properties. Our Complaint-Free Record With The Better Business Bureau Makes You Look Good!**

Attorneys Cheatam And Howe
123 Main St.
Any Town, USA

Dear Attorney,

I'd like to purchase your clients' properties.

There are many times during your course of business when a client may need to sell a parcel of real estate -- sometimes quickly, sometimes not so quickly.

My name is David Lindahl and I'm part of an investment group that buys from 5 to 10 houses per month.

The name of my company is Results Home Buyers. Please look us up at the Better Business Bureau, and check our excellent record.

We specialize in the purchasing of residential properties, apartment houses, and land.

We realize that your clients are the lifeblood of your business, and we will always treat them with courtesy and the utmost respect. We are interested in creating win/win situations, and our goal is that you look good at the end of the transaction.

For further information about Results Home Buyers and me, please call me now at 555-5555.

I look forward to our speaking.

Sincerely,

David Lindahl

P.S. – I will be calling you on Tuesday, August 12, to answer any questions that you may have about me and my company, and to ask you some pertinent questions to determine how I can better assist you and your clients.

**To Get the Forms for This Book and A Free Bonus Gift visit**
www.FormsForBook.com

# Has Your Investment Property Become A Headache? I've Got The Cure…

Janet Smith
123 Main St.
Any Town, USA

Dear Janet,

How would you like to get rid of the biggest headache that you have in your life right now? That's right, I'm talking about your investment property.

If you're ready to sell, I'm ready to buy. I'm an investor in your area who specializes in properties like yours…properties with problems.

Have you had enough of your tenants calling and complaining to the city officials and causing you all kinds of problems? Are you tired of making repairs to things that the tenants damage? Don't these people have anything better to do?

Sometimes people buy properties and don't realize what they've gotten themselves into. Sometimes people buy properties knowing what they're getting into, but they just get tired of dealing with it.

I'm ready to give you a fair price for your property if you're ready to sell. Call me now at 555-5555 and I'll rid you of your headache.

Sincerely,

David Lindahl

P.S. – For a quick, painless sale of your property, call me now at 555-5555!
P.P.S. – I'm an investor looking to **buy your property**--I'm not a sales agent looking to list it!

To Get the Forms for This Book and A Free Bonus Gift visit
www.FormsForBook.com

# Who Else Wants To Sell Their Home In Seven Days Or Less?

John Doe
123 Main St.
Any Town, USA

Dear John,

I'd like to buy your house in seven days or less.

That's right, I want to buy your house! I'm not a realtor; I'm an investor who is part of a group that buys between 5 and 10 houses a month, and we are interested in your house.

You just finished listing your house with the realtor and you didn't get the results that you wanted. You had all kinds of people coming through your house, checking out your things and asking questions that were none of their business.

Do you really want to list with another realtor and go through that again?

How can I close so quickly? First of all, I'm going to pay all cash, so I won't have to wait around from some bank to give me an approval, so you can get your money.

I'll need the seven days to check the title and any liens that are currently on the property. If you want more time, then we can delay the closing so you can have as much time as you would like.

Either way, call me now at 555-5555 and consider your house sold!

Sincerely,

David Lindahl

P.S. – For a no-hassle, quick sale of your property, call me now at 555-5555!

To Get the Forms for This Book and A Free Bonus Gift visit
www.FormsForBook.com

# Prices In (City Here) Have Never Been Higher. Is Now The Time To Sell? Don't Miss Out On This Incredible Market! Read On…

Joe Smith
123 Main St.
Any Town, USA

Dear Joe,

Prices in the (City Here) area have skyrocketed! Now may be the time for you to sell your out-of-state property and get maximum cash out. You deserve it!

The trick to becoming wealthy is to buy low and sell high. You were smart when you bought your property. Will you be smart again and sell it at the right time?

Now is the time to sell, and I'm interested in buying. I'm a local investor who buys properties just like yours.

Have you had enough of being an out-of-state landlord, tired of the hassles from your property management company which always seems to be nickel-and-diming you?

How about the vacancies and the repair costs that just seem to get higher and higher?

I'd like to rid you of your problem and buy your property.

Call me at 555-5555 to discuss what a fair market price would be for your property. I can close quickly, or take as much time as you would like. Call me now!

Sincerely,

David Lindahl

P.S. – To get the maximum value for your out-of-state property, call me now at 555-5555.

To Get the Forms for This Book and A Free Bonus Gift visit
www.FormsForBook.com

Real estate agents can be a great source of leads for your deals. But real estate agents can be a fickle group, and getting them to work with you can be difficult.

Real estate agents have one big advantage: They have the Multiple Listing Service at their disposal, with thousands and thousands of houses for sale at their fingertips. It's a wonder that they are all not real estate investors; but to be honest, not many of them understand the investing game.

The problem with real estate agents is that there is a low barrier of entry. If you can fog a mirror, you can get hired to sell real estate. Of course you have to pass the licensing test, but the owners of real estate brokerage companies play the numbers.

The more agents they get into their office, the better the possibility that one of them will actually be successful. Of course, as they struggle during the first few months, they will sell or list a house to a friend or family member. The owners rely on this.

Here's a startling statistic: 75 percent of new real estate agents do not make it past their first year in business! The main reason is it's too easy to get in to the business and too easy to get out. They like the idea of being their own boss, but they forget that it takes work to succeed. They never learn how to discipline and manage themselves.

Realtors come in all shapes and sizes, and all have different ethical and moral values. You may work with some that resemble used-car salesmen, and then you can be working with true professionals.

## Working With New Agents

If you're just starting out, you may want to work with an agent that is just starting out as well. A new agent will be hungry and will be willing to do things that an experienced agent will not, such as presenting lowball and creative offers.

The good thing about working with a new agent is that you can train them to work with your style of investing.

To Get the Forms for This Book and A Free Bonus Gift visit
www.FormsForBook.com

The flipside of working with a new agent is just that--they are new. They won't have the inside track on the bank-owned properties. But if you work with an agent who works for a company that does a lot of bank-owned properties, you will increase your odds.

Another drawback that you may want to consider is that a new agent's negotiating skills may not be fully developed. If they haven't done a lot of deals then their inexperience on how to keep a deal together may hurt you.

But if I couldn't find an experienced agent to work for me, then I would certainly work with a newer one.

## Working With Experienced Agents

Your goal should be to get in with an agent that is doing a lot of deals, is aggressive, has worked with investors, and is working with different banks that have foreclosed properties.

These agents are probably already working with some investors and you will be low on their priority list when you first meet them.

You must "schmooze" them and stay in constant contact with them. They have other investors who are also contacting them for business. Most people contact realtors once or twice and give up.

> ▶ *Follow-Up Fact:* ◀ **Statistics show that it takes an average of four contacts before a person will start doing business with you. This is why you must follow up, follow up, follow up, and then follow up some more.**

Or they sit around waiting for the real estate agent to call them. **Successful people take action.**

Statistics show that it takes an average of four contacts before a person will start doing business with you. This is why you must follow up, follow up, follow up, and then follow up some more.

## How to Find the Agents Doing All the Deals

How do you find the agents that are doing a lot of deals, and listing a lot of houses? Call you local Board of Realtors and ask them for the names of the 25 top listing agents in your area.

When you get the list, pick up the phone and start calling. Introduce yourself and ask if they would be interested in working with an active real estate investor. When he/she says yes, then offer to take them out to lunch so that you can introduce yourself and explain what you're looking for, and how you do business.

Do not go into detail over the phone about who you are and what you do. Your main objective is to get the agent out to the restaurant, so that you can start building a relationship. Before people will start doing business with you, they must like and trust you.

You must get them to like you and it is a lot easier when you have an hour of "face time" instead of ten minutes on the telephone.

When you get them out to lunch, don't come across as some "nothing down, seminar graduate." If you don't have any money, you should forge partnerships with "elephants" (people with experience and money), private money or hard money.

If you've got a local real estate investment club in your area, join it. It's a great place to find financing for your deals. You find clubs in your area simply by going on the National Association of Real Estate Investors website. Click on your state and a list of clubs in your area will appear.

The last thing a real estate agent wants to do is present an offer for no money down.

After the lunch, follow up with a phone call and a handwritten note.

To Get the Forms for This Book and A Free Bonus Gift visit
www.FormsForBook.com

When the agent starts giving you addresses of properties, go out immediately and determine whether or not they are deals and get back to the agent with an answer as soon as possible. For the ones that are not a deal, explain to the agent why you can't make the deal work, as this will help them specify what you are looking for.

If you take your time looking at the properties and don't get back to the agent in a timely manner, he/she will simply go to the next investor on his/her list and you will probably never again get the chance to be on top.

# Important Tips to Keep Agents Sending You Houses

Here are some other tips when working with experienced agents:

- Tell them you don't need them at the home inspection.
- Tell them that you don't need them at the closing.
- Do as much running around for them as you can.
- If it's a vacant property, do the walk-through without them.

> ▶ *How To Make Agents Hand You Deals:* ◀ **The more you do for the agent, and the easier you make their job of selling houses to you, the more that they will want to work with you.**

The more you do for the agent, and the easier you make their job of selling houses to you, the more that they will want to work with you.

## Should You List With an Agent to Resell?

One of the ways that I am able to get experienced agents to work with me is to give them the listing to resell the property after the work is done.

Sure this costs me money (between four and seven percent commission); but I factor that into the deal at the beginning when I'm figuring out all of my costs, and when I'm deciding how much I can pay for the property.

You have a better chance of getting that agent's business if you offer the resale because they are going to make more money from you. They will get the commission from the sale of the property to you and the sale of the property when you sell.

If you were an agent and you had a list of investors to call after you just listed a hot deal, whom would you call first? Of course, the person from whom you're going to make the most money.

Later on, if you were that agent and you had multiple offers in on one of your hot properties, whose offer do you think you might lean towards when presenting the offers to the seller? Of course, the one that will make you the most money.

## Why You Shouldn't Try to Get the Lowest Commission From a Realtor

I've heard some investors tell me that they have a real estate agent that only charges them two percent to list their property. That's crazy, and here's why:

This is how real estate agents are trained when they have a buyer:

- Find out buyer's criteria for a home;
- Match buyer's criteria with all homes on the market;
- Show buyer first three homes that match his criteria;
- Show homes that pay the highest commission first;
- If buyer doesn't buy, show next three homes, highest commission homes first;
- If buyer doesn't buy, show next three homes, highest commission first.

Real estate agents are in business for themselves and so are the brokers for whom these agents work. Their first priority is to stay in business. Therefore, brokers train their agents to find all of the houses that match the buyer's buying criteria and then to show them in the order of highest commission first.

So if you are getting a cut-rate commission from your agent, he's not doing you any favors because your house is not going to get shown as much. Here's the formula that you should be concerned about:

**Higher commission = more showings = more offers = a higher price paid for your house in less time**

It's as simple as that. You should be paying whatever the average is for your area. In my area right now, it's five percent. If I really want to move a house quickly, I'll put it on for six percent.

As long as you account for the commission at the time you're figuring out your costs during the buying process, your profit margin will be where you want it to be.

> ▶ *Don't Go Cheap On Commissions!* ◀ **As long as you account for the commission at the time you're figuring out your costs during the buying process, your profit margin will be where you want it to be.**

# Costly Mistakes to Avoid When Working With Real Estate Agents

Don't renege on an offer. If you put an offer in on a property and it passes your home inspection, then you had better close on that property. If you don't, you will never get another deal from that agent.

You see, that agent is counting on that money to feed his family. When you don't close on the deal, you have just taken food off his table and he/she will not forgive you.

To Get the Forms for This Book and A Free Bonus Gift visit
www.FormsForBook.com

So do all of your due diligence up front and when you sign that contract, <u>close on that deal</u>.

Real estate agents can be a great source of income and can help your investing career quickly. I know an investor that does over 50 houses per year, and she gets almost all of her deals through real estate agents.

If you're in an appreciating market, it's harder to get deals from real estate agents because there are not that many good deals out there. Besides, first-time home buyers will pay more than an investor for houses that need work. But that doesn't mean there are no deals from real estate agents to be had.

There are, and always will be, so add real estate agents to your successful marketing mix.

## A Letter Campaign for Real Estate Agents

Want to contact a lot of real estate agents all at once? Why not send them a letter?

Get a list of all of the agents from your local board of Realtors. At the end of this chapter there is a letter that you can use to get realtors to call you.

When sending out the letter, make sure that it is on your company letterhead. You want it to look as professional as possible.

Be sure to sign it in blue ink. If you have someone else addressing, licking and stamping your envelope, also have them sign your name. You don't have to sign it yourself. They don't know what your signature looks like and this is not a legal document.

Have the envelope address handwritten with blue ink and have a return address on the envelope. I would just put the address, no company name and no P.O. Box. Use your own home residence if you have to.

Make sure you use a live stamp; do not use a postage meter

To Get the Forms for This Book and A Free Bonus Gift visit
www.FormsForBook.com

These are all tips to help you get your envelope opened and read. The more letters that are read, the more business you will get.

Look at the bottom of the letter. It states that you will be following up with a phone call. This will increase your business phenomenally! Be sure to do it at the date that you say you will.

Make that date no more than a week after you send the letter, and use the fact that you said that you were going to call them as the reason for your calling. The dialogue should go like this.

"Hi Mary Realtor? It's Dave Lindahl calling from Results Homebuyers, I'm following up on a letter I sent you a couple of days ago. I stated in the letter that I would be calling you today to discuss my proposal in the letter. Did you get a chance to read the letter?"

If they say yes, begin the discussion, "Then as you know, I'm a real estate investor looking to purchase problem properties. How many addresses of properties do you have that I might be interested in?" Then just wait and continue the natural flow of a conversation.

After you do this a few times, you will begin to get really good at it.

If they say that they didn't receive the letter, don't let that bother you. Simply say, "Oh, I'm sorry to hear that…well in the letter it explained that I'm a real estate investor and that I'm looking for houses that have problems. Do you have or know of any houses that have little equity, that are just plain ugly, that need a lot of repairs or maybe are getting close to foreclosure? I buy houses just like that and I'd like to work with you in finding them. Are you interested in increasing your income?"

Then go on to repeat, in your own words, what the letter says.

Some will work with you, some won't. Don't get bothered if you call a few and you don't get anywhere. It only takes one or two good real estate agents to make you a lot of money, so it's well worth getting a lot of "no's" to get the big "YES!"

To Get the Forms for This Book and A Free Bonus Gift visit
www.FormsForBook.com

Nine out of 10 real estate agents won't work with you. So what does that mean? You have to call at least 10 agents! If you want three or four agents working with you then you've got to call 30 to 40 agents.

It's all just a numbers game. Play the numbers and you will be a big winner!

Real estate agents should be a part of your overall marketing plan, but you should not rely on them for all of your business. But by following all of the concepts in this manual, you won't have to.

> ▶ *It's All A Numbers Game...* ◀ Some agents will work with you, some won't. Don't get bothered if you call a few and you don't get anywhere. It only takes one or two good real estate agents to make you a lot of money, so it's well worth getting a lot of "no's" to get the big "YES!"

# I Want To <u>Buy</u> Those Listings
## That You Just Can't Seem To Sell!

Agents Name
Company
Address

Dear (Agent's Name),

Getting hounded by a seller whose house you can't sell? Getting close to the expiration date of one or more of you listings? Is a foreclosure date coming fast and you're worried that you're not going to get paid for all of your hard work?

I want to buy those houses so that you get paid your commission! My name is (your name here) and I'm a real estate investor. I'm associated with a group of investors who buy anywhere from 5 to 10 houses a month. We can pay cash, close quickly and we'd like to take your problems off your hands.

Do you have any houses that:

- ✓ There's not enough, little or no equity to cover the mortgage or the real estate commission?
- ✓ Are approaching foreclosure?
- ✓ Need a lot of repairs?
- ✓ Are just plain Ugly?
- ✓ Are in a War Zone?

Or do you know of any? I want to buy those houses and get you your commission. Whether it's on the listing side or the buying side, I want to work with you to make you more money.

Of course, anything I buy I will need to resell, and I like to resell my properties with an agent with whom I have a working relationship and I'd like that agent to be you!

If you have or know of any properties that would be a match for me (basically anything that is a problem) please pick up the phone and call me now at 555-5555. Otherwise, I will be calling you next Tuesday to see how we could possibly begin a lucrative relationship for both of us.

Sincerely,

(Your Name Here)

P.S. – Please don't prejudge what I might be interested in. I'm not a "wanna-be" real estate investor. I buy all kinds of houses, in all areas and in any condition. I have multiple purchase plans available and an unlimited supply of capital.

P.P.S.- Isn't it time that you get paid for all those deals you worked so hard on, that didn't sell? Call me now at 555-5555.

## To Get the Forms for This Book and A Free Bonus Gift visit
### www.FormsForBook.com

# *Chapter 6*
# **Buying Right**

Contrary to popular belief, you don't make your money when you sell your house; you make it when you buy it.

A lot of rehabbers get into trouble because they fail to take into account what all of their expenses will be prior to purchasing the property. Because of this, they pay too high a price and start losing money before they even begin the rehab.

The most common mistake that rehabbers make when purchasing property is to figure out what the rehab will cost, add in their profit and come up with an offer. Do this often enough and you will be out of business before you even begin. What they are doing wrong is that they are not taking into consideration the rest of the cost that they are going to encounter during the purchase, rehab and sale process.

The following is the process, or system, that you should use every time you consider purchasing a new property. If you follow this process entirely, you will considerably lower the risk of buying a property at too high of a price.

## **Determining Your ARV**

The first thing you need to do is to determine your after repair value (ARV). This is how much money you will be able to get for the house, based on the current market, after you have done the repairs.

This is done by conducting a market analysis. When doing a market analysis, you want to compare your house with houses that are the same style and size that have sold in the area in the last six months and have sold within one-half to two miles from your property. You also want to take into consideration houses that are currently under agreement but have not closed, and houses that are currently on the market for sale.

To Get the Forms for This Book and A Free Bonus Gift visit
www.FormsForBook.com

Houses currently on the market are the houses that you will be competing against if your house were ready to be put on the market today. Of the three, they are the least reliable when determining price. Anyone can put a house on the market for any price, but the key question is, will it sell? Do not value your house solely based on what is currently on the market.

Although this can be an indication of where the market is heading, it's when a buyer comes forward and puts his hard earned cash down to make the purchase that value is determined.

You can get this information from the Internet at the following sites: Realtor.com, How Much Is My House Worth.com…

Sometimes a real estate agent will do a market analysis for you. Be careful. The real estate agents income is a result of you buying the property, not you making money on the property. They may at times have a tendency to be a little (a lot!) optimistic on what you may able to get for the property when it's time to resell.

Always take the properties that they compared your property against (called comps) and ride by them. Make sure that they are in yours or a similar neighborhood, that they are the same size (gross living area is one of the key pieces of information that a bank appraiser uses to determine value), and are the same style.

Compare amenities, such as: do they both have garages, fireplaces, basements, the same lot size, the same number of bathrooms and bedrooms? Most of this information will be on the property sheets that the real estate agent gives you. If they are different, which all houses are, you have to determine how this affects value.

Here is a general rule of thumb: add or subtract $10,000 for a bedroom, $2000 for a fireplace, $15,000 for a garage, $20,000 for a basement, and $10,000 for a bathroom.

# Figuring Out Your True Cost

As I said, just figuring out the amount of work that needs to be done and adding in your profit is no way to determine how much you will pay for a property. You must consider all costs associated with the property and then come up with a figure that will be your maximum allowable offer (MAO). MAO is the absolutely highest price that you will pay for a particular property.

If you exceed your MAO during your negotiations, then you are setting yourself up for failure. Most people that exceed their MAO do so because they have gotten themselves emotionally wrapped up in the deal.

# Negotiating Money Making Tip

Always be prepared to walk away from a deal. Do not get emotionally attached to any property. Often times it is the deal you walk away from that is the best deal that you make.

People tend to get emotionally attached because they've done all the research, worked all the numbers; they see themselves doing work on the house; they see this house repaired; they see themselves driving by with friends with chin held high saying, "Yep, I own that one;" they see themselves selling it to the new homeowner; and, most of all they, see themselves sitting at the bank with a big smile on their face and a big check in their hands, making a big deposit.

They **want** this deal!

They've been looking and looking and finally… finally they found a house to buy.

Here's the best advice I can give you. Be prepared to walk away from negotiations at any time. He who cares least wins. If you get emotionally attached to a deal, you've already lost. You may pay too much for the house and you may end up out of the money before you even get started.

To Get the Forms for This Book and A Free Bonus Gift visit
www.FormsForBook.com

Do not exceed your MAO.

Here is how to determine what the MAO will be on any given house.

First, you need to take into consideration <u>all</u> of the expenses that you will incur while you have ownership of this property, which include:

- ➢ Attorney fees to purchase
- ➢ Attorney fees to close
- ➢ Financing fees
- ➢ Real estate commission
- ➢ Taxes
- ➢ Water and utilities
- ➢ Rehab cost
- ➢ Insurance
- ➢ Interest
- ➢ Profit

Let's go over them one by one. Prices will vary from city to city, state to state, these are estimates.

### Attorney Fees and Settlement Charges To Purchase

You or your lender will have to have a title search done to make sure that the current owner has a clean title. The attorney will also charge you for miscellaneous "junk" fees like overnight package fees, notary fees, funding fees and recording fees. These fees could range from $1,000 to $3,000.

If you are taking ownership in the form of a Trust or a Limited Liability company -- which you should do to protect yourself and your assets (if you're not sure what I'm talking about, speak to a good Real Estate Attorney and he will fill you in) -- you will be charged anywhere from $750 to $1,500 to set up the entity.

### Attorney Fees and Settlement Charges When You Close

When you close you will have to have a new deed drawn up to pass along ownership to the new buyer. You will have recorded a discharge of mortgage if you didn't buy the property with all cash. The

To Get the Forms for This Book and A Free Bonus Gift visit
www.FormsForBook.com

attorney may charge you for overnight fees to pay off your lender. Any outstanding water and taxes owed to the city or town will be paid off at the closing, and you may see a bunch of little miscellaneous "junk" fees from your attorney on the settlement statement.

Most states charge some sort of excise tax when you sell a property. My state charges 4.56 percent of the sales price. Find out what your state charges.

All in all, these fees may run you anywhere from $1,500 to $2,500.

## Financing Fees

If you are not paying all cash for the property, you will be obtaining some form of financing. If you use a conventional bank or mortgage company, that bank may charge you points. A point is one percent of the loan amount. If you're borrowing $75,000, one point would be $750. Banks charge zero to three points.

If you are using a "private" lender -- a lender (usually a wealthy individual) who specializes in quick real estate loans, who doesn't care much about your credit and is primarily interested in whether you have entered into a good profitable deal -- that lender will typically charge five points.

Banks or mortgage companies usually will charge you additional fees for the following: plot plan, title insurance, processing fee, underwriting fee and discount fee. Depending on the institution you use, you may get hit with a bunch of "junk" fees. Banks are usually more lenient with junk fees, mortgage companies usually hit you, while "private" lenders will only charge you for any actual out-of-pocket costs they incur.

For banks and mortgage companies, these fees average $1,500 to $2,500.

## Real Estate Commissions

If you are going to sell the house yourself, you will not see this fee. If you are new at real estate investing, you may want to consider a worst-case scenario, that you won't be able to sell it on your own and put some money here just in case.

Typical real estate commissions range from four to seven percent of the purchase price. In my area a safe number to use is five percent. Do not go for the absolute lowest commission that you can find. Real estate agents work on commission. They usually split the commission down the middle between the listing agent and the selling agent. When a selling agent is showing houses to their prospective client, you'd better believe that they are showing them the houses with the highest commission first.

If their buyers don't like any of those houses then they go to the next level of commission. By paying a little higher than average commission rate, there is a higher probability that more prospective buyers will see your house, and because of that there is a higher probability that it will sell faster and for a higher price.

Selling faster reduces your carrying cost, and selling for higher puts more cash in your pocket. The extra money that you will receive by getting both of these results usually exceeds the extra amount that you paid in commission. There is one more benefit -- you get your money back faster so you can go onto the next deal!

### Taxes
Assume that you will be carrying this house for six months from purchase to sale. Take the yearly tax bill and divide it by two.

### Water and Utilities
You're going to be using water and electricity when doing the repairs on the house. You may need to use gas or oil to heat the house while you do these repairs. After the repairs are done you will continue to use electricity and maybe heat to show it to prospective buyers.

When making this estimate, you've got to consider the time of year it is when you are buying the property. If you are buying in September, you will be holding the house (assuming six months) throughout the winter months. Your heating bill is going to be a lot higher than it would if you were holding through the summer months.

To Get the Forms for This Book and A Free Bonus Gift visit
www.FormsForBook.com

I usually estimate $75 a month for water and utilities. Six months would be $450.

If I'm heating a house during the winter months, I figure on $200 per month and then adjust accordingly to the time of year.

### Rehab Cost
In the following chapters, I will show you how to figure out your rehab costs. You will insert that figure here.

### Insurance
You will be insuring a vacant house that is under construction. Insurance companies have a special program for this situation. They call it the "pool." They usually write the policies for three to six months, and they tend to be pricey. They do not like to insure these properties.

Regardless of the cost, you need the insurance. I have had two properties catch fire while under rehab, and one property had a "freeze up," in which all of the water in the house froze and burst all of the pipes, then it thawed and poured water all over the house!

Don't make the mistake of getting a regular homeowners insurance policy. If you have a claim and the insurance company determines through their investigation that the property was vacant (they do a very thorough investigation) they will not pay the claim. I know of two investors in my area that this has happened to.

In my area it costs me $800 - $1,200 for a six-month policy. Check with the insurance agent in your area.

### Profit
The best for last! After figuring out all of these costs, can you believe that some investors do not put in an allowance for profit! They figure that they will make their money by selling the property in a shorter time frame, or thinking that they can actually do the rehab for a lot less than what they calculated.

At the end of this chapter you will find a form that I have devised that you can use when calculating your MAO. It's called the Calculation

Worksheet and Budget form. If you follow the steps on this form each time you are analyzing a property, you will be sure not to miss any important costs.

I also use this form as a budget tool as well, to make sure that my costs are in line with my estimate while I'm doing the rehab. At the end of the rehab, I fill in what my actual costs were. This helps me to understand where I am weak on my estimations -- and if I didn't obtain the profit amount that I had anticipated -- where those profits went so that I can watch those costs more carefully during the next rehab.

If you notice near the bottom of the page, there is an item called Total Daily Carrying Cost. This is the amount of money that your property is costing you every day! I keep it posted where I can see it to give me a daily kick in the pants to get my property done.

You calculate this figure by adding your yearly (take any of your figures and convert them to yearly figures) taxes, insurance, utilities and interest and divide this number by 360.

Always put in for a profit. It is the reason we are in this game. I won't go into a rehab unless I am going to make a $20,000 profit. If it's going to be a big rehab, over $25,000, then I want a $30,000 profit.

Some people who are just starting out will work for a $10,000 to $15,000 profit. That's fine, but just remember, it's a very rare occasion when a rehab project comes in on time and on budget. It doesn't take much for a project to go out of whack. Once it does, the money from your profit will be paying the extra cost. That is why I like to have a cushion of at least $20,000.

Here's an example of some common mistakes that beginning investors make. Joey and Mary Wannabuy have an opportunity to purchase a three-bedroom ranch in a good section of town. Tom and Nancy Needtosell answered their We Buy Houses sign that they saw on the side of their car.

The Needtosells told the Wannabuys that they were getting transferred and wanted to sell their property.

To Get the Forms for This Book and A Free Bonus Gift visit
www.FormsForBook.com

The Wannabuys did a market analysis on the property and determined that its after repaired value (ARV) was $110,000. The house needed some work. The Wannabuy's figured that the rehab would be approximately $12,000.

They wanted a profit of $15,000. They didn't want to appear greedy, but in actuality were too timid to demand more. (After a couple of deals, you will have no problem commanding $20,000 profit per deal.)

They figured that they would sell the house on their own, thus saving the real estate commission. They were sure that they were accurate on their rehab cost of $12,000 but wanted to have a cushion so they upped their estimate to $14,000.

They figured that, since the property was in a good area and the rehab was not that big, they would have the house fixed and sold within three months. They figured their interest on a loan amount of $65,000 (plucked out-of-air), they would get their money from their bank using a "no point" mortgage, thus saving them on closing costs. The interest rate is 10 percent. The monthly payment would be $571, amortized over 30 years (P = 65,000, I = 10 percent, N = 30).

Since they would have the loan for three months, this would equal $1713. They figured miscellaneous closing costs would be another $1,000.

So they figured out their MAO as follows:

| | | |
|---|---|---|
| ARV | 110,000 | |
| | | |
| Rehab | 14,000 | |
| Mortgage Payments | 1,713 | |
| Attorney and Settlement costs | 1,000 | |
| Profit | 15,000 | |
| Total | 31,713 | |
| MAO | 78,287 | |

They offered the Neetosells $75,000 for the property. They accepted and the Wannabuys were thrilled because that meant that since they bought below MAO, they would make even more money.

Six months later, the property finally sold. The rehab took longer than they had expected. They didn't start setting up the contractors before they closed, so there was a delay in getting started on the job. When they finally got going, a few problems arose which they took care of, but it delayed the completion of the rehab by a month. The total cost came in at $17,000 instead of $12,000.

The Wannabuys thought they had a buyer for the house only to find out three weeks into the mortgage process that the buyer could not qualify for the loan. They decided that it would be easier to sell it with a real estate agent this first time to make sure that they had a qualified buyer so that they wouldn't have to go through that mess again. Besides, they wanted to close and get their profits!

They agreed on a five percent commission.

The agent sold the house to a buyer at $110,000, and in the sixth month it closed.

Here is how the numbers looked at the closing:

| | |
|---|---|
| Sale Price | 110,000 |
| Purchase price | 75,000 |
| Realtor Commission | 3,750 |
| Rehab | 17,000 |
| Interest Payments | 3,426 |
| Attorney Fees and Settlement Charges Purchase | 3,800 |
| Attorney Fees and Settlement Charges Closing | 980 |

| | | |
|---|---|---|
| Insurance | | 800 |
| Taxes | | 452 |
| Water and Utilities | | 475 |
| | Total | 104,683 |
| | Profit | 4,317 |

The good news is they made a profit of $4,317, the bad news is they thought they were going to make $15,000. I guess they won't be going on that cruise they had planned with the profits, but hey, anytime you make a profit in this business it's good news. Then what you do is review the entire deal, figure what you got hung up on, find a way to do it better, so in the next deal you will make even more money.

In this case, the Wannabuys didn't take into consideration some very standard costs, such as water and utilities, insurance, realtors fees (always add them in, even if you don't use one you can show this to the seller to get a lower price), attorney's fees and settlement costs at closing. And they didn't realize that the only loan that they could get was a construction loan.

This is because since the house was in need of repair, the bank considered it an incomplete house and would only give construction financing. You almost always have to pay two points with construction financing, and you will see a slew of "junk" fees. In the Wannabuy's case the total was $3,800.

The rehab came in $5,000 over budget, actually $2,000 over budget if you account for their cushion. You should always use a cushion. I usually add 10 percent as a "fudge" factor. Your rehab will almost always come in over budget. Almost always!!

Had the Wannabuys factored in all of these costs before determining their MAO, they would have realized that their actual MAO was $64,317.

| | |
|---|---:|
| ARV | 110,000 |
| Realtor Commission | 3,750 |
| Rehab | 17,000 |
| Interest Payments | 3,426 |
| Attorney Fees and Settlement Charges Purchase | 3,800 |
| Attorney Fees and Settlement Charges Closing | 980 |
| Insurance | 800 |
| Taxes | 452 |
| Water and Utilities | 475 |
| Profit | <u>15,000</u> |
| Total | 45,683 |
| | |
| MAO | 64,317 |

The only cost that they still would have been a little over on was the rehab, which brings us to the next chapter: How to accurately determine your rehab cost to keep your losses at a minimum and keep those "chunks" of profits accumulating in your bank account.

# Offer Calculation And Budget

Property
Address_____

|  | **Actual** | **Proposed** |  |
|---|---|---|---|
| **Sales Price** | _____ | (After Repaired Value) | _____ |
| Rehab | _____ | | _____ |
| Closing Cost – Purchase | _____ | | _____ |
| Closing Cost – Sale | _____ | | _____ |
| Insurance | _____ | | _____ |
| Taxes and Water | _____ | | _____ |
| Utilities | _____ | | _____ |
| Interest Payments | _____ | | _____ |
| Broker's Commission | _____ | | _____ |
| Profit | _____ | | _____ |
| Other | _____ | | _____ |
| **Sub Total Cost** | (_____) | | (_____) |
| **Purchase Price** | | **MAO** _____ | |
| (_____) | | | |

**Total   Profit** (calculated after house has sold)

_____

**Total Daily Carrying Cost**
(Yearly taxes, insurance, utilities, and interest divided by 360)$ _____

Issues_____.____
_____
_____
_____

# Chapter 7

# Property Inspection Checklist

The next six pages contain the Property Inspection Checklist that I have used in almost every one of the over 400 rehabs that I have done. I found out early that if I didn't work off of a checklist, I usually missed a couple of things that ended up costing me money and lowering my overall profits. One of the keys to running a successful business is to systemize everything.

Many times when you are walking through a property, you may see a big problem in one area of the house that sets your mind racing with thoughts like, "How will I fix that problem? How much will it cost? Who can I get to do that for me." While these thoughts are racing through your mind, you're supposed to be inspecting the other parts of the house and now you're more likely to miss other things. You can increase the odds that you have accounted for all of the repairs if you work off this checklist.

Let me give you an example of what happened to me once. I got a call from a man who had an old New England Colonial farmhouse that he wanted to sell. He had lived there for over 50 years and now he was old and it was time to move on. He hadn't done much maintenance in those 50 years, and the repairs on the house had gotten way ahead him.

This place needed a lot of work! The exterior needed painting, the roof sagged, which meant there were rotted decking boards below the shingles (a big job), and the interior hadn't been updated since the 1950s. This house needed everything.

As he gave me the tour of the house, I was quickly awestruck by the place. It was rich with history. Built in 1742, it was the original house for a very large farm that was run by a wealthy landowner back in the revolutionary days.

To Get the Forms for This Book and A Free Bonus Gift visit
www.FormsForBook.com

Every room had a fireplace, as this was central heat back then. It had the big hearth fireplace in the old kitchen, now the living room, where all of the meals were made. The fireplace was very deep so that a large black kettle of food could be hung.

There were no windows back then, and the windows had the original shutters that would slide in and out of the wall -- one on each side. In the center of each shutter was an opening in the shape of a small cross. This cross wasn't there because they were Christians, this cross was there so that they could stick their muskets out and shoot at any attacking Indians! It was absolutely fascinating.

The tour concluded in the basement where there was a very rare brick beehive oven, which was used for baking bread. As a person who loves to cook, I could only imagine the sweet smells emanating from the different types of breads that would have been baking there.

Needless to say, I bought the house. When I completed my estimating, it looked like it would need about $66,000 to get it back into shape to resell it.

The project was going along fine and very close to budget, until one day I received a call from my foreman, who said, "Hey Dave, what are we going to do about these rotted beams?"

"What rotted beams?" I asked. I didn't remember any rotted beams, I looked at my notes and there was nothing about beams.

"You don't know about these beams?" he said. I could hear the surprised tone in his voice. "You'd better get over here."

I hopped in my car and met him at the site. Sure enough, in the midst of me fantasizing about all that bread baking in that oven, I never looked up and inspected the beams and floor joists. Seventy-five percent of all of the beams and floor joists had been destroyed by powder post beetles, a common insect in New England that eats wood from the inside out and is very similar to termites.

They all either had to be replaced or re-enforced at a cost of $22,000.

I didn't have a Property Inspection Checklist that day. If I had, my MAO would have been $22,000 lower!

So, to keep as much money in my pocket as possible, I developed this checklist. Since I've been using it, it has yet to fail me.

Review the following pages. When you're done, continue on, and I will explain how to determine the cost of each of the categories

# Property Inspection Checklist

**Property Address** _____

## Clean Out
Interior _____ $_____
Exterior _____ $_____

**Total Clean Out**    $_____

## Wallpaper/Sheetrock/Mirrors
Drywall Repair_____ $_____
Drywall Replace _____ $_____
Wallpaper Repair _____ $_____
Wallpaper Removal _____ $_____
Mirrors _____ $_____
Other _____ $_____

**Total Wallpaper/Sheetrock** $_____

## Interior Paint
Touch up _____ $_____
Doors Only _____ $_____
Walls Only _____ $_____
Ceilings Only _____ $_____
Total House _____ $_____
Other _____ $_____

**Total Paint**    $_____

## Carpentry In/Out
Interior Doors_____ $_____
Exterior Doors _____ $_____
Interior Trim _____ $_____
Cabinets _____ $_____
Door/Cabinet Hardware _____ $_____
Counter Tops _____ $_____
Windows _____ $_____
Screens _____ $_____
Siding Repair/Replace _____ $_____

Exterior Trim/Siding _____ $_____

Fence _____ $_____

Garage Doors _____ $_____

Gutters _____ $_____

Shutters _____ $_____

Other _____

_____

_____

**Total Carpentry** $_____

**Property Inspection Checklist**

**Electrical**

Fixture Repair/Replace_____ $_____
Ceiling Fans_____ $_____
Outlet/Switch Repair/Replace_____ $_____
Globes/Switch Plate and Outlet Covers _____ $_____
Wiring Repair/Service Upgrade_____ $_____
Breaker Repair/Replace _____ $_____
                            **Total Electrical** $_____

**Plumbing**

Toilet Repair/Replace _____ $_____
Faucet Repair/Replace _____ $_____
Sinks _____ $_____
Showers – Tile _____ $_____
Tubs – Tile _____ $_____
Grouting/Caulking Tub/Shower _____ $_____
Interior Pipes _____ $_____
Exterior Pipes _____ $_____
Winterization/Dewinterization _____ $_____
Other _____ $_____
                           **Total Plumbing** $_____

**Appliances**

Range _____ $_____
Vent Hood _____ $_____
Cooktop _____ $_____
Oven _____ $_____
Dishwasher _____ $_____
Disposal _____ $_____
Refrigerator _____ $_____
Other _____ $_____
                           **Total Appliances** $_____

## Heating/Air

Condenser Repair/Replace_____ $_____

Furnace Repair/Replace _____ $_____

Thermostat Repair/Replace _____ $_____

Duct Work/Grills _____ $_____

Water Heater _____ $_____

Oil Tank Replacement (**have owner remove old if underground!!**)

_____ $_____

Other _____ $_____

       **Total Heating/Air**  $_____


## Exterior Paint

Doors Only_____ $_____

Trim Only _____ $_____

Siding Only _____ $_____

Total House _____ $_____

Other _____ $_____

     **Total Exterior Paint** $_____

## Roofing

Replacement _____ $_____

Repair Leak/Flashing _____ $_____

Decking _____ $_____

Other _____ $_____

       **Total Roofing**  $_____

## Flooring

Carpet Replace _____ $_____

Carpet Cleaning _____ $_____

Vinyl Replace _____ $_____

Vinyl Repair _____ $_____

Subfloor Repair/Replace _____ $_____

Tile Repair/Replace _____ $_____

Hardwood Floor Refinish _____ $_____

Hardwood Floor Repair _____ $_____

Other _____ $_____

      **Total Flooring**  $_____

## Structural

Foundation _____ $_____

Posts and Beams _____ $_____

Grading _____ $_____

Masonry _____ $_____

Engineering Inspection _____ $_____

Driveway _____ $_____

Other _____ $_____

**Total Structural** $_____

## Exterior

Landscaping _____ $_____

Mailbox/Numbers_____ $_____

**Total Exterior** $_____

## Other

_____ $_____

_____ $_____

_____ $_____

_____ $_____

_____ $_____

**Total Others** $_____

# Total Estimate of Repairs $_____

# Flooring Estimate

| Room Total Sq Ft | Flooring Type | L x W |
|---|---|---|
| _____ | _____ | _____ |
| _____ | _____ | _____ |
| _____ | _____ | _____ |
| _____ | _____ | _____ |
| _____ | _____ | _____ |
| _____ | _____ | _____ |
| _____ | _____ | _____ |
| _____ | _____ | _____ |
| _____ | _____ | _____ |
| _____ | _____ | _____ |
| _____ | _____ | _____ |
| _____ | _____ | _____ |
| _____ | _____ | _____ |
| _____ | _____ | _____ |
| _____ | _____ | _____ |

**Total Sq Ft**      **Carpet** _____

**Total Sq Ft**      **Vinyl/Tile** _____

**Total Sq Ft**      **Hardwood** _____

# Formulas and Measurements: Flooring

**Carpet**

| | |
|---|---|
| Total number of square feet | A) _____ |
| Divide A by 9 = | B) _____ |
| Multiply B x 1.05 = | C) _____ |
| Multiply C times price per yard installed | |
| $ _____    D) _____ = Cost of carpet | |

**Vinyl/Tile**

| | |
|---|---|
| Total number of square feet | A) _____ |
| Divide A by 9 = | B) _____ |
| Multiply B x 1.05 = | C) _____ |
| Multiply C times price per yard installed | |
| $_____    D) _____ = Cost of vinyl/tile | |

**Hardwood floors**

| | |
|---|---|
| Total number of square feet | A) _____ |
| Multiply A by price per square feet  $_____ | B) _____ |
| Number of closets | C) _____ |
| Multiply C times price per closet $_____ | D) _____ |
| Number of stair treads | E) _____ |
| Multiply E times cost per stair tread $ _____ | F) _____ |

Add B+D+F                                              G) _____ =

Cost of refinishing hardwood floors

# Formulas and Measurements: Exterior

## Painting

Length x width _____  =  _____
Length x width _____  =  _____
Length x width _____  =  _____
Length x width _____  =  _____

Total        A) _____
Price per sq ft $ _____ x A  = $_____

Cost of Exterior Paint

## Vinyl Siding/Roofing

Length x width _____  =  _____
Length x width _____  =  _____
Length x width _____  =  _____
Length x width _____  =  _____
Total                      _____
Divide total by 100    _____ X price per square
$_____

Total        $_____

## Soffit/Facia
Total Linear Feet     _____
X price per linear foot      $_____

         Total    $ _____

## Gutters
Total Linear Feet     _____
X price per linear foot      $_____
         Total    $_____

# Property Inspection Room By Room

## Property Address_____

Room Description _____ Size _____
Flooring Type _____
Doors _____
Lt/Ceiling Fans _____
Drywall Repair_____
Paint Hours _____
Wall Paper _____
Other _____
_____

Room Description _____ Size _____
Flooring Type _____
Doors _____
Lt/Ceiling Fans _____
Drywall Repair_____
Paint Hours _____
Wall Paper _____
Other _____
_____

Room Description _____ Size _____
Flooring Type _____
Doors _____
Lt/Ceiling Fans _____
Drywall Repair_____
Paint Hours _____
Wall Paper _____
Other _____
_____

Room Description _____ Size _____
Flooring Type _____
Doors _____
Lt/Ceiling Fans _____
Drywall Repair_____
Paint Hours _____
Wall Paper _____
Other _____
_____

Room Description _____ Size _____
Flooring Type _____
Doors _____
Lt/Ceiling Fans _____
Drywall Repair_____
Paint Hours _____
Wall Paper _____
Other _____
_____

Room Description _____ Size _____
Flooring Type _____
Doors _____
Lt/Ceiling Fans _____
Drywall Repair_____
Paint Hours _____
Wall Paper _____
Other _____
_____

Room Description _____ Size _____
Flooring Type _____
Doors _____
Lt/Ceiling Fans _____
Drywall Repair_____
Paint Hours _____
Wall Paper _____
Other _____
_____

# Property Inspection:
# Exterior

**Roof**

_____

_____

**Windows**

_____

_____

**Screens**_____

**Siding**

**Repair/Replace**_____

_____

**Paint**_____

_____

**Woodwork**_____

_____

_____

_____

**Lighting**

_____

**Underground Oil Tank**

_____

**Landscaping**

_____

**Gutters**

_____

**Masonry**

_____

_____

**Clean up of Debris**

_____
_____
_____

# Other:

_____
_____
_____
_____
_____
_____
_____
_____
_____
_____
_____
_____
_____
_____

# *Chapter 8*
# Property Inspection and
# How to Determine Cost

As you can see, the Property Inspection Checklist is very thorough. As long as you follow the checklists and perform the different calculations as stated in the worksheets, you'll be on your way to accurately figuring out your repair costs and MAO. The following prices are estimates. Prices differ from city to city, state to state.

To estimate the repairs for a property, quickly review the Property Inspection Checklist so that you have a good feel for what you're going to be looking for when you inspect the property. Then take out the Property Inspection Room x Room sheet ( I bring up to six blank copies with me) and go through the property room by room, noting all of the repairs in each room. A pantry, hall, breezeway, foyer and any other area that needs attention is considered a room on these sheets. Be sure to note next to the room description what type of living area you're looking at.

Next, go outside and walk the grounds with the Property Inspection Exterior worksheet. Note any repairs that need to be made on the appropriate areas on the sheet.

When you have inspected the inside and the outside of the property, pull out your Property Inspection Checklist and review it once more to make sure that you didn't miss anything.

Now it's time to go home (or to the office) and make some calculations.

Take out the completed Property Inspection Room x Room sheet and the Flooring Estimate Worksheet. Transfer all of the flooring from the Room x Room sheet to the Flooring Estimate Worksheet. As you transfer

To Get the Forms for This Book and A Free Bonus Gift visit
www.FormsForBook.com

the flooring from the Room x Room to the Estimate Worksheet, cross it off on the Room x Room sheet.

Each time you record the information from the Room x Room sheet onto another sheet, put a line through it. At the end of your estimate, when you've made all of your transfers, you can quickly scan all of your Room x Room sheets to make sure that everything has been crossed of.

This insures that you have not missed anything. You know what happens when you miss something….lost profits.

Calculate your totals for all of your different flooring types at the bottom of the page. Next, transfer those totals to the Formulas and Measurements Flooring worksheet. Follow the steps and do your calculations (you will find the different labor and supply cost to use in your estimates as you read through the following chapter). When you have completed your calculation, transfer this number to the Property Inspection Checklist. You have just completed the flooring component of your estimate.

Next, review all of your Room by Room pages for anything that has to do with cleaning out the property. Transfer this information to the "Clean Out" section of the Property Inspection Checklist, and cross out that item on the Room by Room list.

Do not total up the items until you have transferred all of the information from the Room x Room sheets. When all items have been crossed out on the Room x Room sheets to the Property Inspection Checklist, then move on to your Property Inspection Exterior form.

From your Property Inspection Exterior form, transfer the information to the Property Inspection Checklist, using the Formulas and Measurement Exterior worksheet when applicable.

Now that all items have been transferred from the Room x Room sheets and the Property Inspection Exterior form, it's time to begin calculating costs. You'll find the cost of supplies and labor for every one of the items on the Property Inspection Checklist as you read through the rest of this chapter.

To Get the Forms for This Book and A Free Bonus Gift visit
www.FormsForBook.com

Later in this Manual, you will also find a case study, which is broken down into two parts. All of these forms are filled out and the calculations are completed for a house that we are presently looking to buy.

Starting from the top of the Property Inspection Checklist form, I'll briefly describe each of the items on the form and show you how to estimate each of their costs.

## Clean Outs

Once, we filled seven 30-yard dumpsters while cleaning out a property. That's enough trash to cover two football fields! While we were doing it, we found some really great stuff, like a trunk full of Norman Rockwell collectable plates, over 50 Kennedy silver dollars, antique chairs and much more.

And once, while cleaning out a dark cellar, my partner grabbed what looked like a big, wide, crooked rug leaning against a dark corner. The rug said, "What are you doing?" and my partner screamed and ran out of the cellar. Apparently, some junkies had gotten into the house the night before and what we thought was a rug was actually a person left over from the party.

If a clean out looks like a big job, you'll want to get a dumpster. They come in 10, 15, 30 and 40 yard sizes.. Make sure that you don't rent one that has a weight restriction, which is how the dumpster people increase their fees. They will allow five tons (or something like that, it depends on the company and the size of the dumpster) of debris and anything over that is extra.

You've got to calculate the time you think it will take to do the job in man-hours. Put a price on those man-hours), add the dumpster cost and you have your estimate.

When loading a 30 or 40 yard dumpster, don't just throw the debris over the sides. Open the door at the end and walk the junk into the dumpster and pile it neatly. You will be able to get a lot more into the dumpster this way, thus saving you money.

Every town has their share of junk men. They usually advertise in the local paper, the penny saver papers, or on the side of their truck. If you can't find one, call the local fire department, because someone there will know one.

These men usually perform clean outs at a reasonable cost because they are actually going to make money on the junk. They will pick through it and sort it as if they were looking for a needle in a haystack. If only they were taught to look for investment properties like this, someone else would be carting off **their** junk!

If my crew is not going to do the job, I will call two or three of them and get bids. The lowest bid wins, it's as simple as that.

I combine the interior and exterior when I do my estimate for a clean out. When inspecting the property, don't forget to look in crawl spaces, attics, lofts in garages, behind garages, and on the outskirts of the property if it abuts woods, sheds, pool houses, as well as under porches. If you don't, you'll be sorry.

I have forgotten to look in each one of these places at one time or another and each time the area was packed with debris! You would be amazed at how much junk people can stuff in a small area.

After we complete our job and all of the repairs are done, I always send in a cleaning girl to spruce the place up. The house should already be pretty clean because you should insist that the workers leave the work area clean every night.

If you don't, the place will quickly look like a dump and at any time a potential buyer could be in the area and ready to walk through the property. Opportunity favors the prepared.

To Get the Forms for This Book and A Free Bonus Gift visit
www.FormsForBook.com

# Wallpaper/Sheetrock/Mirrors

### Drywall Repair

I walk around the house and each hole in the wall I see that is the size of a fist (literally), I figure it's going to cost me two man hours to repair.

When filling a hole that is deeper than an inch and wider than two inches by two inches, you should fill that hole with a filler first. Sometimes we use newspaper. If you don't, when you put a thick amount of drywall compound on an area that has some depth, it could take between two and three days to dry, and it usually dries with a big crack down the center. You should add the drywall compound in layers. Fill the bottom of the hole first, let it dry, add some more, let it dry, and so on until you get flush with the wall. Then sand the last coat.

When patching a bigger hole in a wall that is drywall, you can do one of two things. You can draw a square around the hole with a ruler (or something with a straight edge) and cut out the square. Place plywood strips behind the opening inside of the wall, and drive screws into them from the front to hold them into place. You can only do one at a time since there will be nothing holding the other one up. Cut your patch to size, put it into place and drive the screws through your patch and into the plywood strip backers. Cover the joints with wallboard tape and finish with compound.

The other method is to determine where the studs are in the wall (they should be every 16 inches), cut the drywall back to halfway on the stud on each side. You may be creating a much larger hole but sometimes this method is easiest. Cut your drywall patch to size and drive screws through the patch and into the studs. Cover with tape and compound.

Older houses have walls made of thick horse-hair plaster. When repairing a plaster wall, make sure that there are no loose pieces of plaster in the hole or still attached to the wooden lathing backing that runs behind the wall. Check the wall in the general area of the hole. If it's loose or spongy, cut the opening bigger until you have a strong secure wall. You may end up with a much larger hole, but you will have prevented more of the wall from giving way later thus causing more repairs. A loose wall will start to give way when you do you carpentry repairs and the banging and vibrating begin.

You want to be sure that the sides of the hole are firm. Use a liquid latex bonding agent that will help prevent cracking and will help adhere to the sides of the hole. When filling larger holes in plaster, the layered approach of adding a layer of compound covering the bottom of the hole, letting it dry, then adding another layer….works best.

If I'm replacing entire sections or walls then I estimate it at $4 per square foot. A drywall contractor will have to install the new drywall, tape the seams, mud the seams and screw holes and sand the seams, then come back and mud and sand again. Sometimes they even come back for a third time. Take this into consideration when you are planning the timing of a job. You don't want to be painting any other parts of the house while there is dry wall work going on, unless you have secured the area with plastic because that dust will get everywhere and will stick to your wet paint and ruin your paint job. So have patience and do things in their proper order. You'll learn more about sequencing in a later chapter.

**Wallpaper Repair**
There are two types of wallpaper repair that I will do. The first is to fasten down lifting seams. This is done by squirting adhesive behind the seam and pressing it back into place. The second is to repair a bubble by slicing it down the middle (as straight as possible), squirting adhesive behind it and pressing it back into place.

If the wallpaper is ripped, torn, has crayon or marker over it, has a lot of holes or just plain looks ugly, I take it down and paint the room a nice neutral color.

Wallpaper removal can be deceiving. It can take a lot longer than it looks. There are two kinds of wallpaper exterior. One has a nice paper exterior that is usually easy to remove. Just spray with some warm water that has some vinegar added, and it usually peels right off with a wallboard knife. Be careful not to make gouges in the wall behind the paper. If you do, you will have a lot of drywall repair to contend with when you repaint.

The other type has a nasty vinyl exterior. This is harder to remove, though sometimes you get lucky and you can literally grab a corner and peel the top layer right off. This will leave you with a paper bottom layer, which you can remove with warm water. If you have a top layer of vinyl that will just not give, you must score (make scratches) the vinyl, then spray it with the warm water and vinegar solution, let it seep in and then attempt to remove it using the drywall knife. This will take you twice as long as paper exterior wallpaper.

Removing wallpaper in a 12 foot by 12 foot room will take about six hours with two people. Factor about a day and a half if the wallpaper has the vinyl exterior..

### Mirrors

This is where I put my estimate for the replacement of bathroom mirrors or medicine cabinets. If the bathroom currently only has a mirror that needs replacing, I replace it. Costs vary on size.

Replacing medicine cabinets without lighting will cost two man hours plus materials. Lighted cabinets will cost more.

Remember, kitchens and baths sell houses. You don't want to get the most expensive mirror or medicine cabinet, but you do want to get the best looking one for the best price. Do not go cheap. No one wants a drug store-looking bathroom, they want comfort and warmth.

## Interior Paint

Paint comes in several finishes and qualities.
The types of finishes are:

a. Flat
b. Satin
c. Eggshell
d. Semi-Gloss
e. Gloss
f. Enamel

I use different finishes for different areas, and I will explain which ones and why as I go along.

To Get the Forms for This Book and A Free Bonus Gift visit
www.FormsForBook.com

The types of paint qualities are:
      a.  Contractor's Grade
      b.  Medium Grade
      c.  High Quality Grade

Do not use the Contractors Grade for two reasons. The first is that although you may be more attracted to it because it has the lowest price, it is very thin and does not cover well (meaning that you will have to use twice as much paint to cover the same area). Therefore you are not really saving.

The second reason is "paint boogers." Cheap paint has a tendency to dry in very small clumps and float throughout the paint. The dried up paint gets on your roller and then onto the wall. When the paint clumps dry onto the wall they make the wall look ugly, like the wall is full of boogers. So we call them "paint boogers."

Before you know it, you're going around the entire house sanding off and touching up "paint boogers." This wastes a lot of time.

When painting the interior of a rehab, it's a good idea to choose neutral colors. Lighter, neutral colors make the rooms look bigger. I have always used a light beige paint for the walls, a color that resembles a light brown eggshell. The type of finish I use for the walls is flat. Flat is the least costly of the choices and it is common to have it on the walls.

For the trim and doors (if they are not stained natural) I use semi-gloss white. This combination really stands out. It makes the rooms look big and clean and it is very pleasing to a potential buyer's eye.

For the ceiling I use a color called ceiling white. It always comes in a flat finish. Don't try to get creative and paint the ceilings a different color other than white, like off white, blue or black. (Yes, I have seen black ceilings!)

Anything other than white makes the room look smaller. Smaller rooms equate to less value in the buyer's mind. Less value means a lower offer -- or no offer at all!

To Get the Forms for This Book and A Free Bonus Gift visit
www.FormsForBook.com

I use a very unique method of estimating how much the interior painting will cost. The following calculations are based on a room that is approximately 12 feet by 12 feet. If the room is smaller than 12 feet by 12 feet, I **do not** adjust down, if it is bigger I adjust upwards.

In my experience of actually doing interior painting, plus timing my crews while they were doing the interior painting, I have found that the following holds true:

It takes approximately one hour to trim out a room. This does not mean painting the trim. This means painting the areas that you have to paint with a brush instead of a roller because the roller cannot get at these areas.

These areas include around window frames, door frames, where the wall meets the ceiling, and anywhere the wall ends and something else begins. Usually it is an area where one color of paint stops and another color begins. You trim this area because you need to be extra careful not to get the wrong color paint on the wrong area.

It takes approximately one hour to use a roller and roll the four walls of a 12 foot by 12 foot room or a hallway.

It takes approximately one hour to roll a ceiling.

It takes approximately one hour to paint the trim on a window frame or a door frame.

If the window has grids, it takes one hour to paint those window grids for one window.

It takes approximately half an hour to paint a door.

It takes approximately one hour to paint a closet.

| | |
|---|---|
| To trim a room | 1 hour |
| Four Walls | 1 hour |
| Ceiling | 1 hour |
| Paint window or door trim | 15 minutes each |
| Paint a window w/ grids | 1 hour |
| Paint a door | ½ hour |
| Paint a closet | 1 hour |

Knowing these numbers, I go through each room one by one and add up the time. First, I count an hour for the ceilings and walls, then an hour for the trim. Then I count the windows, and if there are two then I add a half an hour. Then I count the closet for an hour, and then count the doors. In this case there are two in the room, or one hour.

Of course if I am not going to paint the doors or trim or anything else in the room, I will not count it. The reason that I will not paint something is either the wood is natural or the paint is already in excellent condition and it is the right color.

The above room would take me four and a half man-hours to complete.

Here are some things to watch out for:

a) If the room has paneling, and it is a nice quality paneling, I may decide to keep it on the wall. If it covers half the room then I only put down one half hour for that room for the walls. Generally I will remove the paneling because paneling tends to be dark and this makes the rooms look smaller and projects a gloomy image. If there is not a wall behind the paneling then I will consider the neighborhood. If it is a good to very good neighborhood, I will remove it and install sheetrock. If it is a good to not so good neighborhood, I will paint over it.

b) If the room is very big, then I will add an extra hour on.

c) Texture surfaces take a lot longer to paint, I add half an hour for each wall or ceiling that has a textured surface.

d) If you are going to paint kitchen cabinets, they can take up to two days. You've got to remove every door and remove all of the hardware. The areas are too tight to roll so everything has to be done with a brush. Always use enamel when painting kitchen cabinets.

e) These numbers are based on one coat of paint. If you are painting over a very bright color or paneling, you will want to use a product called Kilz or Bin Primer Sealer as a first coat. These are specialty paints that lock in that underlying color so that that color doesn't bleed through your final coat.

f) If you do not use one of these products then you may have to put on three coats of paint instead of two. I know this by experience.

g) If you are ever painting over wood, use a primer sealer to paint over the knot holes. Otherwise they will all bleed through.

So, if you have to use more than one coat adjust your figures accordingly.

When I am painting a house or if I am hiring someone to paint, I give a value of $25 per man-hour when calculating my figures.

If I have counted up 57 man-hours of painting to be done in a property, then I figure the labor will cost me $1425 (57 x $25).

Based on my experience, when calculating how much paint, the average 1400 square foot house (assuming one coat of paint) uses 10 gallons of flat for the walls, five gallons of ceiling paint and three gallons of semi-gloss for doors, windows and trim. At an average price of $20 per gallon, that would be an additional $360.

I buy the paint in five gallon buckets. It's cheaper this way. I even buy the semi-gloss in five gallon buckets even though I only need three gallons. I just put the extra in storage and use it for the next job.

The total painting estimate for this job will be $1425 plus $360 equals $1785.

I've broken up the Interior paint category on the Property Inspection form into miscellaneous sub categories. Eighty percent of the time, when I paint the entire interior of the house, it just looks better. If on those rare occasions you can get away with either touch ups, doors only, walls only, ceilings only or a combination of those, I have separated those categories for you. This separation lets you know where your head was at when you were estimating this job.

To Get the Forms for This Book and A Free Bonus Gift visit
www.FormsForBook.com

Sometimes you make an offer and it is rejected and two months later you get a call back and they change their minds and accept. This Property Inspection sheet will let you have a quick review of the house as you saw it when you first went in. Of course you will have to re-inspect because time always changes things!

# Carpentry In/Out

When you find a good, reliable carpenter who will work for a reasonable rate and finish in a timely manner, treat him like gold, because they are a rare breed. Carpenters all have their specialties. Some can only do light carpentry work like installing doors and repairing woodwork (i.e. soffits, fascias, decking). Some do light work and can also figure out the installation of a deck system but not much more. Some, although they can do more, only specialize in cabinetry work. Others specialize in roofing and a select few can do finish work and have the end result look professional.

Find out what your guy specializes in. Beware, they will all tell you that they can do everything! There are carpenters that can do everything, but not many.

O.K., let's go down the list.

### Interior Doors
When replacing interior doors, you should match the existing doors in terms of style and material. Interior doors come in three different material types: wood, lueon (hollow or solid) and Masonite. The different styles are either flat or paneled.

When replacing wood doors in older homes, sometimes you will not be able to match the doors, simply because they don't make that style anymore. Just try to match as close as possible and make sure you use wood.

Hollow core lueon doors are very common in bedrooms, hallways and baths in most houses these days. They are made with two panels of lueon held to together with a thin layer of wood on the outside edges, and are separated by strips of heavy cardboard glued on its edges running throughout the middle. This is why you see so many holes in lueon doors, because there is literally nothing in the middle to stop the impact of a fist or a thrown object.

Because the outside edges have only a strip of wood, you can't cut more than one-half to three-quarters of an inch off of these doors when installing them. So if the size you need is not in stock, don't get the next size up and expect to be able to cut it down like you would a wood or solid core lueon door.

Here's another tip, when cutting the bottoms of a lueon door, you will want to use a special blade that they make for cutting lueon. If you're at the job and you don't have one of these special blades, then take off your ripping blade from your skill saw and put it on backward. Cut the door with the blade rotating backwards. It works great. If you don't, your door will splinter badly and look awful.

Another way to prevent splintering is to duct tape the edge that you are cutting, cut it and then take the duct tape off. This method works very well also.

If you are replacing wood doors with lueon doors, the easiest thing to do is to install a pre-hung lueon door. A pre-hung door is just that, a door that is pre-hung in its frame and the best part is, the trim work is already installed as well. You just need to remove the old door and frame and pop in the new one.

A solid core lueon door is usually used for cellar entries or exterior doors for apartment units going into a common hallway. I have seen them used as an exterior door in houses. Although the door is a cheap alternative to wood or metal, it does not hold up well against the weather.

Solid core lueon doors are just that -- solid. The exterior layers are lueon and the interior is firmly pressed particle board. They are very sturdy and can be cut down to any size. Do not put you blade on backwards to cut this door. The wood is solid. You do not need to use the duct tape to eliminate splintering.

Masonite doors are the new kid on the block. Although they look good because they are usually shaped into six panels and are usually white, they are basically made out of pressed cardboard. The same holds true with a masonite door as with a lueon door, the outside edges keep the door together, the middle is filled with strips of cardboard glued on edge. When cutting, use a special blade or take your ripping blade and put it on backwards. Like a lueon door, they also come pre-hung.

### Exterior Doors

Exterior doors come in either wood or metal. Some have windows (called "lights") and some do not. It depends on your preference, but I like to use a door that has a small row of three windows at the top of the door.

The most commonly used exterior door is a metal door. They come pre-hung because you will not be able to cut the door down to size. You will have to adjust your opening to fit the door.

Wood doors come in all shapes and sizes; the most common is a six-panel wood door. Since they can be cut down to size, you really don't need a pre-hung door.

### Storm Doors

If you have a metal interior door, you do not want to install a storm door. The windows on the storm door create a greenhouse effect and may cause the metal to buckle (and will definitely cause the plastic around the windows on the metal door to melt out of shape). I see this time and time again.

Storm doors come in a wide variety of styles. They are not difficult to install and even come with instructions. Remember, since this is the first thing that the potential buyer will touch when entering your house, you want it to look good!

To Get the Forms for This Book and A Free Bonus Gift visit
www.FormsForBook.com

I like to use storm doors that are mostly glass and then paint my exterior door, whether it is wood or metal, a nice warm color. This creates a nice pleasant greeting for the potential buyer.

### Interior Trim

This is just the basic trim. If you want the fancy stuff, then price it at the store before you estimate it.

### Exterior Trim

A very common problem is the rotting out of the corners of facia, soffits and rake boards. Since these boards have the greatest exposure to the weather, they are the first to break down. Fortunately, you don't have to replace the entire board, you can have your contractor cut off the rotted section and replace with a new piece. With some good caulking and some paint, no one will know the difference. There's an old saying that goes like this, "Compound, caulk and paint, make a carpenter what he ain't."

A rotted piece can be cut out from the middle or off the end. It doesn't matter where it is. You will not have to replace the entire board.

### Cabinets

I've said it before, I'll say it again, "Kitchens and baths sell houses." Do whatever you need to do to make those cabinets look good! Sometimes you can get away with painting them, not often, but sometimes. When you do, paint them white! White will make the kitchen look bigger and cleaner. Use an enamel finish. Painting cabinets takes a lot longer than you think. To do it right you have to take of all of the doors and remove all of the hardware. There are a lot of nooks and crannies in cabinets that take time to paint. You can't use a roller because off the space limitations and the fact that most cabinet doors are raised paneled, plus the shelving takes a long time to paint.

If you are painting over a finished surface, you must lightly sand the surface so that the paint absorbs in and sticks. Otherwise it will peel very easily. If the cabinets are not already white, you should use a primer sealer.

Painting the average set of cabinets will take one man two days.

To Get the Forms for This Book and A Free Bonus Gift visit
www.FormsForBook.com

The only cabinets I paint are already painted cabinets or old pine cabinets.

If the cabinets need replacing, you can get good, quality construction grade cabinets at Home Depot or any of the box stores. Try to keep cabinets a light color, like a light oak or even a white laminate. I usually use the light oak. This helps make the kitchen appear bigger.

If you're not sure how to layout your cabinet, measure out the interior room dimensions and put them down on a piece of paper. Then measure the distance from each door and window to the nearest wall. For example, there is usually a window over the kitchen sink. Measure the left side of the window edge to the left wall and measure the right side to the window edge to the right wall. Make sure you measure the width of the window or door as well. Do this with all windows and doors.

Next, set up an appointment with the associate at Home Depot that handles kitchen layouts (don't just walk in, they work by appointment), give him your dimensions, and he will help you figure out a cabinet layout. Do this a couple of times and you'll be figuring it out for yourself and calling your order in.

To install kitchen cabinets, a contractor will probably charge you per cabinet. If it's a really small job, you may be charged a minimum rate.

If you have the contractor supply the cabinets and do the work, it will cost you more money because he will mark up the price of the cabinets. This is a standard procedure. You've got to decide if the increased cost will justify the amount of time that you will save by not having to deal with supplying the cabinets.

If you're replacing the bathroom vanity you, can usually get a deal on a combination set -- a vanity plus sink in one. Most vanities come in 24 to 36 inch lengths. If possible, your vanity should match your medicine cabinet. If you are replacing both, it's easy to match. If you have a good, quality medicine cabinet already in place, get a vanity that will go well with it.

## Countertops

Countertops can be difficult. If you have the standard "L" shape counter top, then you can pick up the counters at Home Depot or any of the box stores for a good price.

If you have a custom countertop, then the best thing to do is to remove the existing countertop and bring it to your local countertop maker to see if it can be resurfaced. Resurfacing will save you a lot of money. When they resurface, they simply install a laminate right over the existing countertop, and it looks as good as new.

If it can't be resurfaced because it's too damaged, then he can build you another one and use that one as a template. That way you know that you have the right measurements, thus avoiding the possibility of someone making a mistake and having the wrong countertop built.

## Door/Cabinet Hardware

Sometimes all you need to do is replace the hardware on a set of cabinets to spruce them up. When you're replacing cabinets, don't forget to account for the hardware. Typically, when replacing old or installing new, you'll need 20 to 40 pieces of hardware. At $5 each, this will cost anywhere from $100 to $200 for the material. If you don't put this in your estimate, this will come right off your profit. It's the little things that add up to gobble up your profit.

Here's a tip: Cabinet hardware is usually fastened on with either one or two screws. So, when you take the old hardware off, you will have either one or two holes in the cabinet door. When buying new hardware, buy hardware that will match the existing hole structure, that way you will not have to do any more drilling and you will save time and money. Sometimes you find hardware that fits your kitchen perfectly but it has the wrong hole structure, **don't buy it**! You're not going to live there. Save your money for yourself!

When inspecting a house, you may see missing doorknobs, also called "handsets.". Count up the number of handsets that need to be replaced and add them to your estimate. Another little thing that can add up to a lot if you don't put it in.

To Get the Forms for This Book and A Free Bonus Gift visit
www.FormsForBook.com

## Garage Doors

You can have a garage door replaced for approximately $800 per door. If it's an extra wide door, then the price would go up to $1,100.

Does it have a garage door opener but you don't have the clicker? Go to your nearest electronics store with the brand name of the door opener and get a universal garage door opener. If the door opener works, great. If it doesn't then you can either replace or remove the existing one. A replacement will cost $200 to $250.

## Fencing

You should consider installing fencing if you are trying to block the view of something unpleasant like an adjacent lot that is filled with unsightly debris, or if the house abuts a commercial property that has a lot of trucks. Otherwise you would just need to do a repair.

If you're installing to block a view, you will want to use stockade fencing. It comes in a height of six feet and is eight feet long. You can either get spruce or cedar. Spruce is the least expensive and looks just as good. A fencing contractor will charge you $40 to $50 per section to install. Each section is eight feet long.

## Siding

Siding comes in many different varieties, such as clapboard, stucco, cedar shingle and vinyl. I'll cover each one of them separately.

Clapboard siding is usually found on high-end houses. If replacement is needed, it is usually because of water, and it's usually due to a gutter without a downspout that continuously pours water down the side of the house (thus rotting the siding).

Replacing the clapboard siding is not difficult if the rot is within reaching distance from a standing position. If it is higher on the house, then it becomes more difficult. The higher it goes, the more difficult it becomes because of the positioning of the ladder.

The replacement boards will cost about $8 to $10 per linear foot and then you will pay for the contractor's time. Take into account that you will have to have the wood primed and painted as well.

When repairing cracks in stucco siding, simply clean the crack with a wire brush, use a calking gun and fill the cracks with concrete caulk, overfill slightly and smooth to the surface. Let dry and paint to match.

Patching small areas can be done with a premix stucco mix. Remove loose area with a wire brush, apply premixed stucco with a putty knife or trowel, and texture the repaired area to match the surrounding surface.

Larger areas should be done by an experienced contractor. The hardest part of the job is getting the right mix between the dry stucco mix and water. The wrong mix usually results in a sloppy job. The job will be estimated by either one-half day or full day (four hours or eight hours) plus materials. Expect to pay $25 to $45 per hour for labor. Materials may run $50 to $100, depending upon the size of the job.

### Cedar Shingles
Cedar shingles come in either a white cedar or a red cedar. White cedar is least expensive and is the most commonly used. If treated properly, cedar shingles last about 20 years. The problem is, if you are looking at a house in which the shingles are starting to curl or they have shrunk and there are very wide spaces between them, the home inspector is going to tell the new buyer that they need to be replaced.

If this is the case, you will have to strip them (take the old ones off) to install the new ones. Replacing cedar shingle siding is estimated by the square. The average cost per square is $250 to $300, not including the stripping. Add an extra $100 per square to strip.

You may only have a section that needs to be replaced. Many times the north side of the house will weather faster than the other sides and the shingles on this side will need replacing. Or maybe one of the downspouts has been pouring water onto a certain section of the house for a long period of time, thus rotting out the siding.

Estimates are done in the same way, by the square. If it is a smaller job, the price per square will be higher because the contractor will want to earn a minimum rate.

Replacing missing shingles is an easy job and the price you get to do this should reflect this. If you have a couple of missing shingles it may cost you $65 for a minimum rate. If you have a lot, then figure you will be charged by the hour at $25 per hour plus minimal materials cost.

### Vinyl Siding

Once you strip those shingles, you don't have to reapply new ones. You may consider installing vinyl siding. Vinyl siding can cover a number of problems. You may consider vinyl siding over a paint job where paint is peeling badly; of for one that has already been painted over a couple of times and the previous owners did it without scraping the wood work. Thus to scrape off the two layers of paint and paint chips would be so time consuming that it would probably be cheaper to put vinyl siding on it.

At one time they were using pressed wood to side houses. This material didn't really hold to the weather that well, and the results were that the edges of the boards would rot. This is also a good candidate for vinyl siding replacement.

Vinyl siding is priced by the square and the extras that you may want done. It will be your option to vinyl side the soffits and facia and the window trim. Get prices for all before you make a decision.

The price per square, just for the siding will cost $125 to $175. Soffits and facias, depending upon difficulty and height, will be priced per linear foot at $5 to $10 per foot.

Vinyl repair is not difficult. Simply unlock the interlocking joints of the vinyl siding, cut out the damaged area and install the new. It gets a little tricky to nail in the new piece, you'll want to use a pry bar to lift the siding and a hammer to drive the nails home.

The hardest part of the repair will be to match the existing siding. You may have to buy a box (one-third of a square) just to get the piece you need.

## Windows

Old double-hung windows with the old weight system in the walls are drafty and will scare your buyers away. Not only that, trying to find missing windows for your storm window systems is nearly impossible. You usually have to replace the entire storm window.

If you have the old double hung windows, you should put in budget to replace them. The new vinyl clad, insulated windows can be bought for $100 to $200 each. The beauty is that you will not need a storm window. You could get the cheaper wood windows for $50 to $75 each, but you will need a new storm window for these and those storms will cost about $35 to $50 apiece, so you're at the same price. Anew buyer will feel much more secure with the vinyl clad windows.

Vinyl clad windows are very easy to install. A window can be done in 20 to 30 minutes by an experienced contractor.

If you are measuring for your windows, make sure you measure from the inside of the window casing from the top to the bottom and from side to side. The common mistake is to measure from the outside of the window sash, from side to side and up and down. Your windows will come in too small, and you will have to spend time and material to build your window opening down to fit your new window.

However, too small is much better than too big, because if you order your windows and they come in too big, there's nothing you can do but eat the mistake. You can't build the window opening any bigger. You could but it will cost you a lot in labor cost. If you're lucky, the window company may take them back if they are a standard size, but if they are an odd size, put them in storage and wait until another job comes up where you can use them.

The best thing to do is to have the window company representative come out and do the measuring. That way if there are any mistakes, they made it and they will eat it.

To Get the Forms for This Book and A Free Bonus Gift visit
www.FormsForBook.com

The normal fee for window installation is $35 to $75 per window. If you are replacing the old double-hung windows with the weight system, make sure the contractor is going to take that weight out of the wall. It's in the wall in a hidden compartment on each side of the window. Make sure he is going to fill that cavity with insulation. If he doesn't, the insulation effect of the window will be no good because the air will either come in or escape through these cavities.

If you have to repair the glazing (fix a broken window) of an insulated window, you have to remove the sash and take it down to the glass store so that they can repair it. You can't do it yourself because it is insulated glass. Let them know a couple days in advance that you will be coming so that they can do the job on the same day. A repair of an insulated window will cost between $90 to $150! Almost the same as a new window, but not quite.

If a window appears foggy or moist, this means that the seal is cracked and you will have to replace this window as well.

Look around for miscellaneous single panes of glass that need to be replaced and add them to your estimate. This is another one of those little things that add up to be a profit gobbler if you don't account for them.

Replacing a sliding glass door will cost about $800 for the new door and $300 for the installation.

If the seal is cracked or one side of the insulated window is broken, the repair will cost about $300.

### Screens
If you are missing some screens, the home inspectors will pick up on it. Replace them at $20 to $30 each. You can have them made to size at any window company.

### Gutters
In the old days, all houses had wood gutters. Each year or two you would have to treat those gutters with linseed oil to prevent the water from

penetrating the wood and rotting the gutters away. This chore could be daunting due to the fact that you had to climb a ladder and hang over the side to brush the oil on. Because of this, many people did not keep up this maintenance and the wood gutters rotted through.

Usually when the gutters rot through, the soffit (the board that lies parallel to the roof) and the facia (the board that the gutters are attached to) rot through as well. When you are estimating a gutter repair or replacement, keep this in mind.

Replacing wood gutters can be an expensive task. Gutters are sold by the linear foot and although you may not have to replace the whole gutter, even a small replacement can become costly. Wood gutters cost up to $15- $25 per linear foot to install.

Hence the invention of aluminum gutters. Most cities now have companies that will come to the job and make the gutters right there on site. They have the aluminum wrapped up in a big ball in the truck. You give them the measurement that you want and they feed the aluminum into a "bender" and make you a gutter, custom ordered right there on the spot. Of course, they will also supply you with all the fasteners, rivets, downspouts, elbows and sealants and any other accessories that you might need.

Priced per linear foot, custom aluminum gutters will run you about $5- $10.

When installing, make sure you have the proper pitch. Of course it needs to pitch in the direction of the downspouts. If you have one on each end, then pitch it from the middle down to the sides.

If you are doing any vinyl siding work or roof work, be sure to install the gutters last or you just might have to take them down and put them back up.

### Shutters
Shutters really make a house look sharp. You should always have shutters on the front of your house. If there are none there now, buy some and have them installed. They make them out of plastic now in many

colors. Even the plastic ones look great. They are inexpensive and easy to install. All you need is a drill and a hammer.

Standard plastic shutters cost about $15 to $45 a pair. What a bargain. Estimate the hourly rate at $25 per house. A pair take about one-half hour to install.

# Electrical

Any time you are doing a service upgrade, installing panels or running new wires, you should hire a licensed electrician. You could be seriously injured by crossing the wrong wires.

It reminds me of the time when I was installing a dishwasher, lying on the kitchen floor in a condo, late at night, and everyone else had gone home. I made sure that there was no chance of that black wire hitting the white wire, because the black wire is usually live.

Why I didn't just turn the power off I don't know. But I didn't, and as I was moving the white wire into place with my right hand, the black wire, which was an arms length away and on the other side of my body, touched the back of my left arm.

The current arched through my body and sent me flopping on the floor like a fish looking for water. That lasted for about 10 seconds, but 10 seconds is a long time when an electrical current has gotten a hold of you.

The moral of the story is, if you're not sure what you are doing, hire an electrician. A good electrician will cost you $45 to $85 an hour. If it is a small job, they may charge you a minimum of $75 to come out and do the job.

If you don't know a good electrician, go to the local supply store and get a referral. They know all the good ones. Another way to get a referral is to ask another sub contractor that you are currently working with whom he would use.

O.K. let's go down the list:

To Get the Forms for This Book and A Free Bonus Gift visit
www.FormsForBook.com

### Fixture Repair/Replace

Fixtures are easy to replace. You can get decent brass and glass fixtures for between $10 and $45. Don't get too fancy. Just get something that looks good.

### Ceiling Fans

I like to replace light fixtures with ceiling fans. These cost a little more but they really add to the ambiance of the house. A decent ceiling fan will cost you $30 to $70 at Walmart or any of the box stores. It will cost another $50 to install.

### Outlets and Switches

Sometimes I will replace all of the outlets and switches if they look ugly, if they have been painted over for years, or if maybe the wall was once brown and now I've painted it off-white. I want those outlets and switches to match my wall.

If I want to modernize an old house, I'll replace the light switches with those new square ones, which is a great trick and they look great.

Outlets and switches will cost you a couple of dollars each, and they are easily replaced. Make sure you first shut off the power at the fuse box and then attach the wires to the new outlet, or switch the same way they were attached to the old one, or you may reverse the polarity and it will not work.

### Globes and Switch Plates

Globes are the glasswork attached to lighting. If I have a broken or missing globe but the main body of the light is O.K., I'll just replace the globe. This is cheaper and less time consuming. Globes go for $3 to $9 each. Before you go off to the store to pick up new globes, make sure you measure the opening. They come in different sizes and this will save you a second trip.

Switch plates are the plates that frame the outlets and switches. I always replace all of them throughout the house to match all the walls. This is a nice finishing touch that is inexpensive. I've always put down a standard price of $60 to replace them all. This includes material and labor.

To Get the Forms for This Book and A Free Bonus Gift visit
www.FormsForBook.com

**Wiring Repair**

Have an electrician do this and get a bid.

**Breaker Repair/Replace**

Have an electrician do this. It shouldn't be more than $50 to $100 to repair/replace one breaker.

# Plumbing

A lot of people, when they are starting out, do their own light plumbing. It's not that difficult and can save you some money. A good plumber is going to cost you $45 to $90 per hour.

Here's a run down of what different items will cost you:

**Toilet Repair/Replace**

You can replace a toilet for under $250. Don't forget to pick up a wax ring. When you remove the toilet this wax ring goes between the new toilet and the waste pipe. You'll see where the old one was. If you don't replace the wax ring, you will have a leak.

If you don't have to replace the toilet, take a look at the toilet seat, if it is worn at all or doesn't match its surroundings, replace it. You can get a good and inexpensive one for $10. If you want to spend a little more, I've had a lot of positive responses to those cushioned seats and though I doubt if someone will buy the house because of the toilet seat, it will be added to the list of positives in the buyers' mind.

**Faucet Repair/Replace**

Always install quality faucets. Even if the existing one is still functioning. In the kitchen the women will be impressed with a quality faucet, and remember they are usually the ones spending the most time at the sink (not being sexist, it's just a fact). Same thing in the bath. Anything that the new potential buyer is going to touch every day should stand out as special. It's these little things that will help you sell your houses faster and for more money.

A good, fancy faucet will run you $125 to $180 for the faucet only. If you don't install it, add additional money for the plumber.

### Sink

Same thing with the sink, though I don't go out of my way to replace a sink like I do the faucets, if I want to give a little more "wow" to the kitchen, I'll put in a fancy sink. Cost range from $150 to $250. If I am replacing the counters, I always put in a fancy sink.

### Pipes

If you have leaks or need to replace missing or corroded pipes, the easiest thing to do is to call the plumber. Remember, estimate it at about $45 to $75 per hour plus parts.

### Showers

A shower head will cost about $30. The most common problem with a shower is the Symons valve. This valve is what controls the water temperature and the flow and is found in both tubs and showers. A Symons valve replacement will cost around $160-200.

### Tubs

Need to replace a tub? First consider repainting it with the new tub paint that they have out. I have painted over old avocado green and harvest gold tubs with white tub paint with great results, which saves a lot of money on the replacement.

Still need to replace the tub? The easiest tub to install is the two piece and they look great. A plumber will charge you $600 to $800 to do this.

The most common problem around the tub area is loose tile on the wall. What has happened is that the grout has worn away and water has gotten behind the tile and into the wall and has rotted the wall away. You can tell this has happened when you push against the wall and it is spongy.

You will need to have the tile removed, new green board (the type of water resistant material used in bathrooms) installed and then reinstall the tile. These repairs usually run $300 to $1000, depending on the severity.

Sometimes, if the job is too big and it appears that it might get costly, I'll simply buy a tub surround and install it right on top of the tiles. You can get a decent tub surround at Home Depot for about $150. Don't get the cheapest one, remember kitchens and baths sell houses.

A common problem that you will find in tiled bathtubs is missing soap holders. They used to make them with what looked like a handle on the top and what people would do is grab on to the handle when they were getting out of the tub. Doing this enough times with the pressure of a human body, the adhesive eventually gets weak and it comes off.

Don't try to replace these with another soap holder, they don't make them that size any more, just match the tile as closely as possible and install new tile into the area.

### Winterization/De-winterization

When a house is winterized, all the water in the house is drained down, along with the hot water tank and the heating system. The house then sits with no heat on until someone comes along and de-winterizes it and starts using it again.

If you are purchasing a house that has been winterized, request that it be de-winterized so that you can inspect it properly. What usually happens is that the plumber does not get all the water out of the pipes, heating system or water tank, and the water left behind freezes.

When water freezes, it expands, thus expanding the sides of whatever is containing it. This results in split pipes, possible water tanks, and in a worst case scenario, the heating system develops a crack. Once it is cracked it is not good. Big expense. This would occur only in a forced hot water system. A forced hot air system would not have any water in it. If the heating system is cracked, you automatically need a new one. Don't let someone tell you they can patch it. They can't, those patches are very temporary.

You cannot see a crack in a heating unit by looking at the outside. The cracks occur internally. You must fill the unit with water so you can see if it leaks. This is the only way to ensure that you have a good unit.

If you can't have the house de-winterized and you think you've got a really good deal and don't want to lose it, assume that you will have to replace the heating system. Another way to reduce your risk is to inspect the entire copper pipe for splits or blown apart joints. Inspect the corners and joints first, because they will be the first to give way during a freeze up because they are held together by solder and are the weakest link. Then go along the pipes and look for splits. If you can't find any splits and the corners and joints are all intact, there is a good chance that whoever winterized the property did a good job, but this is not a guarantee!

If you have a house that you have completed the rehab, and you find yourself in the winter months and thinking about winterizing it to lower your risk of a freeze up, you may want to think twice.

No matter how good it looks, it is easier to sell a house that is warm and inviting instead of cold and clammy. Also, when you turn the heat off, everything in the house becomes cold. When it becomes cold, it contracts and when your freshly painted walls begin to contract they crack and peel and your paint job is ruined.

Here is one way to reduce your risk. There is a product that I have used that is a thermostat hooked up to the telephone line. If the house goes below a certain temperature, say 50 degrees, the machine automatically calls your home number and gives a warning sound when you pick up the phone. When you hear that sound, you know that you have a problem and you must go to the house right away. If you're not home, it will leave the sound on your answering machine. You can even have it call your cell phone if you want.

This system has saved me a couple of times. One time I didn't have it, and I had a big mess!

A winterization should cost around $200 to $30200. It's less expensive for houses with forced hot air and electric heat for obvious reasons (because they do not hold water!). Have a trained plumber

To Get the Forms for This Book and A Free Bonus Gift visit
www.FormsForBook.com

perform the winterization. Have the same plumber de-winterize the property so that he can fix any mistakes he made during the winterization process. He should fix his mistakes for free. De-winterizing should cost about $0.

# Appliances

If the appliances appear old, replace them. It doesn't matter if they work or not. Again, the old adage rings true -- kitchens and baths sell homes (are you starting to get the message?). If the one who will be doing all of the cooking, stocking the fridge, and loading and unloading the dishwasher is turned off by the appliances, he/she will not buy. Simple as that.

When you purchase the new appliances, find the best "dent and save" in your area. A lot of times you can get good appliances that have minor dents or scratches that you don't even notice and save lots of money! Sometimes you can get good used appliances at the second hand store or in the classifieds in the local paper.

Your appliances should match each other and they should be coordinated with your overall color scheme. If you have beige walls and a beige floor, you should have beige appliances. You could go with black or stainless steel, but these are more expensive. Only go with these high-end colors if the house warrants it.

Let's go down the list and find out what each appliance should cost you, as well as a pointer or two on each:

### Range

This is what the woman or man of the house will cook on. It should be sleek, you do not want the absolute basic model, and a lot of the lower end models look great these days. Do spend the extra money for a self cleaner. A new electric range will run you $500, a "dent and save" maybe $250 to $300.

A gas range is about $50 more, but in most states you will have to get a licensed plumber to install it. Some states, like mine, require that you pull a permit and have the gas fittings inspected after they are installed. If you do it yourself (you shouldn't if your state doesn't allow it), make sure you test for leaks! Simply put soapy water over the fittings, turn on the gas, and if you see bubbles then you have a problem. No bubbles, no problem.

### Vent Hood

This goes over the stove and vents out the range area. You can either get an interior vented or exterior vented system. Find out what style you are replacing and stick with it.

It you have an exterior vented hood vent, you will have duct work coming from the vent hood into the wall and from there it travels up the wall, across the ceiling and out the side of the house.

An interior vented hood vent uses charcoaled filters to do away with the vented air all within the hood vent itself. This is the easiest to to install.

Installation of a basic hood vent costs about $180 including the hood vent.

### Garbage Disposal

This is another item that I usually only replace if there is already one there. To install a new garbage disposal in a kitchen that did not already have one will require a plumber or plumbing skills and an electrician. This can become costly.

If I am replacing the kitchen cabinets and sink, I may consider adding a disposal when I install the new cabinets and sink. With the kitchen already torn apart, it will not cost as much to install a new disposal.

The installation of a garbage disposal is about $150. If you are installing a brand new one when one didn't exist before, the cost is about $240.

### Dishwasher

Every house should have one! If there isn't one already there, I try to find a way to add one. If I am replacing kitchen cabinets, I always add one. Many a deal has been lost because the home did not have a dishwasher. The woman of the house does not want to spend her days doing the dishes.

A new dishwasher installed where there already was an existing one is about $425.

If you are creating a space and installing a new one into an area where one did not exist before, you again get involved with plumbing and electrical, but in this case you may also be required to do some carpentry work because you may be cutting a section out of the cabinets and counter top to make room for the new dishwasher. Take all of this into consideration when looking for a way to get the dishwasher in. Starting from scratch, the installation of a new dishwasher can be between $550 and $900.

### Cook Top
A cook top is just that. Burners, either gas or electric, on top of the counter, with no range below it. Just the cook top. The problem that you will face with these is that the newer ones are not the same size as the older ones,  so you may have do some carpentry to get them to fit. The new ones are usually bigger. A cook top will run you from $350 to $500 **plus** installation.

### Wall Oven
These are the other half of the cook top but are imbedded in a wall in the kitchen. Sometimes, in upscale houses, there are two of them. One on top of the other. If I have to replace a wall oven, I usually try to find a spot in the kitchen where a range can fit. I then remove the wall oven and make shelving, remove the cook top and install a new counter to cover that area. This is the least expensive method of getting this job done, and usually comes out looking good!

If you must replace a wall oven, you'll run into the same problem as with the cook top. They don't make them the same size as they used to. Sometimes they are bigger and sometimes smaller. Whichever, you've got to take this into consideration when you are doing your estimate.

Wall ovens run between $400 and $650 plus installation.

### Refrigerator

If you didn't negotiate the refrigerator when you were purchasing the house, you should have. You'll want to supply a good-looking fridge for the new prospective buyer.

It finishes off a good-looking kitchen. If you have a ratty looking fridge, it can ruin a good-looking kitchen. Get a scratch and dent and save.

If you buy new you'll spend $500 to $800.

# Heating/Air Conditioning

Always verify that the heating system and/or air conditioning system works before you buy the house. If the electricity is not on, have the owner turn it back on, or turn it on yourself, if just for a day, to properly inspect the systems.

If you cannot get the electricity turned on, you should include in your estimate a replacement of the system, regardless of how good it looks. This especially holds true in cold weather climates where the heating system may have cracked during the winter months, and there is no way to tell with a visual inspection.

Always run the air conditioning system to make sure that it is blowing out cold air. If it isn't, it will need a "boost"(about $125), which is an injection of Freon, or there may be a need for further repairs.

Heating systems are typically powered by one of three fuels: gas, oil or electricity. The heating element is usually forced hot air, forced hot water or electric baseboard.

Of the three, the least desirable is electric heat. The main reason is that it is the most expensive of the three heating choices. And buyers know it! In cold weather climates, it is much harder to sell a house that has electric heat. You may want to estimate the replacement of the heating system with either a gas or an oil-fired system. You'll be able to sell the house faster and get more money for it.

To Get the Forms for This Book and A Free Bonus Gift visit
www.FormsForBook.com

O.K., let's go down the list:

### Condenser

This is the unit that powers the air conditioning system. If the air conditioning system is not blowing cold air, get a professional to estimate the repairs. If you think the condenser is no good, a replacement will run you from $1,500 to $2,500.

### Furnace

This is the unit that produces the heat. How do you to tell if you have a forced hot air system? You will have large duct work extending from the system into the floors of the house.

How can you tell if you have a forced hot water system or steam system? You will have copper pipes extending from the system and into the floors of the house. These pipes will go to baseboards or radiators throughout the house.

How can you tell if you have electric heat? There will be no heating unit in the basement, and a thermostat in every room.

How can you tell if you have a gas-fired system? You will see a one-foot round, thick black pipe extending from the heating system, usually extending out the bottom and up the side. This pipe is much thicker than the copper pipes.

How can you tell if you have an oil-fired system? You may see an oil tank in the basement, or on the side of the house if it does not have a basement. Sometimes they bury them in the yard. Never buy a house that has an underground oil tank. (Read more about this under miscellaneous. An underground oil tank once cost me $157,000 to remove!)

Just because you see a tank doesn't mean it is oil-fired. They may have switched to gas and left the old tank there, so inspect the heating unit. There should be a thin copper pipe coming into the furnace from the ground. This is the oil transport pipe. If there is no oil transport pipe and you see a thick black gas pipe, then it probably has been converted to gas.

When estimating the replacement of a furnace, the general rule is that forced hot water furnaces are more expensive than gas furnaces by about $1,000 to $1,500. The replacement of a gas furnace will run you about $2,500 to $3,500. The replacement of a hot water system will be approximately $3,200 to $4,700.

If you are replacing an electric system with a forced hot air system. The entire system, including the duct work, will be around $4,200 to $5,500. Forced hot water systems will be higher by about $1,000.

### Burners
Burners are the little gray or black boxes that hang in the lower front of the furnace. They are the brains of the system. Sometimes you do not need a system replacement; you just need a burner replacement. The replacement of a burner should cost you around $550.

Be careful to note during your inspection whether or not the burner is rented. A lot of people rent their burners from the gas or electric company. A rented burner usually has a gas or electric company sticker on it. Like a rented water heater, you can call the gas or electric company and ask to purchase that burner from them and they will usually give you a good price, depending upon the age of the burner.

### Duct Work/Grills
Inspect the duct work, if there are holes or pieces missing, you will want to repair or replace that area. These repairs/replacements are usually not costly.

Grill refers to the grill that goes on top of the openings of a forced hot air system where the air is pumped into the house. Check to see that they are all in place and if some are missing, add it into your estimate. A grill usually costs from $4 to $10 each.

### Water Heater
The most common reason for replacing a water heater, other than a freeze up, is because the previous owner was renting it from the gas or electric company. If this is the case, before closing, negotiate with the gas or electric company to buy it from them. You will get it for a lot cheaper than having a new one installed.

If you do need to install one on you own, this will cost you between $400 and $900 to have a licensed plumber install it.

### Oil Tank Replacement
If the tank is old and rusting, you may consider replacing it. If it is leaking, you definitely want to replace it. To remove and replace an oil tank that has no oil in it will cost you $700 to $1,500 dollars. If there is oil in it, you will be charged per gallon to remove and dispose of the oil.

### Service Call
Sometimes your furnace just needs a good cleaning. You want to do this before you put the house on the market so that the heating system looks as good as possible. You want to give the buyer a secure feeling that they will not have to replace the heating system in the near future, which is a major expense in the buyers mind and a big deterrent to buying the house. A cleaning costs around $100 and is well worth the price.

# Exterior Paint

The grades of paint are similar for exterior painting of a house as they are with the interior paint. Use a good quality paint as it will cover more evenly and the job will go smoother and faster.

With the new computer matching systems that the paint stores have now, my first instinct is just to touch up any areas of the house that need it.

Whether it be just the trim or the north side of the house (which seems to weather first), I want to do as little exterior paint as possible and still make my house look great from the street. This is curb appeal. If potential buyers don't like what they see when they drive by, it doesn't matter if the inside is like the Taj Mahal, you'll never get them in there to see it.

I always try to paint my front door a warm, inviting color. A color that says to the buyer, "Come in and rest your weary bones, you're home now."

I like to use a light, neutral color for the siding. A dark color makes the house look smaller, a light color makes it look bigger. And, of course, a neutral color to please everybody instead of a just a few or my own personal preferences. I usually use white for the trim.

When determining how long it is going to take to paint a house, you must consider several factors, such as the type of surface; amount of preparation (scraping and priming); whether you're keeping the same color or changing it; and the size and height of the building.

### Type of Surface
Cedar shingles take a lot longer to paint than clapboards. Generally, the wider and smoother the siding, the shorter amount of time it will take you to paint it. The higher the house, the longer it will take to move that ladder and paint it.

### Amount of Prep
Does the house need a lot of scraping? After you have scraped, you will need to cover all of the bare wood with a primer. Do not try to get away with not scraping the house and painting over loose paint. Your paint job will look lousy, defeating the purpose of painting, and it might actually take you longer to do the job because loose paint will be constantly coming off onto your brush or roller and you will have to continuously clean it off.

Sometimes the scraping and priming can take longer than the painting, so plan accordingly.

### Choice of Color
The only time I will change the color of the house is if the original color is too dark, making a small house look smaller, or it is unsightly, such as neon pink. Otherwise, I will keep the same color because I can get the job done in one coat, thus saving me time and money.

### Height of Building
It takes a lot longer to paint the second floor of a building than the first and even longer to do the third. Anytime you have to paint off of a ladder, it is time consuming. You are constantly going up and down and

adjusting and readjusting the ladder. Of course the higher you go, the longer it takes just to get up and down!

In my area (New England) you usually cannot paint from November to March. The weather is just too cold. The surface of the house will not absorb the paint properly, and the paint will not dry properly (called "curing") below 50 degrees.

When this happens, as the weather gets warmer again, your beautiful paint job will begin to peel, usually within six months, sometimes sooner.

In the last couple of years there has been a new product on the market that will allow you to paint at a temperature of 35 degrees and above. We have used it and it works well. It does cost more money, up to $10 more per gallon, so you will have to take this into account when estimating your cost.

There are also specialty paints out now so that you can paint over aluminum siding and vinyl siding. I have done both and the results are great.

In general, the average house will take four to five days to paint. When estimating the cost of painting a house, you will need to calculate the square footage. The average cost of painting the exterior of a house is between $1.50 and $3.50 per square foot.

If you had a Ranch with surface area dimensions of :

|  |  |  |  |
|---|---|---|---|
| 38 x 14 | = | 532 |  |
| 38 x 14 | = | 532 |  |
|  |  |  |  |
| 26 x 14 | = | 364 |  |
| 26 x 14 | = | 364 |  |
| Total Square Footage |  | 1,792 |  |

Total square footage of 1,792 x price per square foot at $2.50 equals total cost of exterior paint at $4,480.

To Get the Forms for This Book and A Free Bonus Gift visit
www.FormsForBook.com

This formula can be found on the Property Inspection Worksheet, Formulas and Measurements, Exterior worksheet.

# Roofing

You must have a good-looking roof on the house, one that does not look like it is on its last legs. A good roof projects security. A bad roof says "danger." A bad roof in a buyer's mind means one thing -- big expenses looming in the near future.

If your asphalt shingles are lifting at the seams this usually means you need a new roof.

Roofs are priced by the "square" (a square is a 10 foot by 10 foot area), and the pitch, or how steep the roof is. The more squares and the steeper the roof, the more it's going to cost you.

If you only have one layer of shingles on the roof, you may elect to do what is called an overlay, which means nailing the new roofing shingles directly over the old ones. If you have two layers of shingles on the roof, most states building codes required that you strip the roof of all the old shingles and start fresh with a new layer. Because you have to strip and dispose of all those shingles, this is the more costly of the two options.

An overlay will cost you between $150 and $250 per square. The steeper the roof, the higher the estimate. A "strip job" will cost you between $250 and $450 a square.

The more valleys and dormers a roof has, the longer it's going to take the roofer to complete the job, and the more he is going to charge you.

When looking at the roof, make sure that there are no sags in the roof line. If there are, you probably have a problem with the decking below the roof surface. You will have to replace this wood and should adjust your estimate accordingly.

To Get the Forms for This Book and A Free Bonus Gift visit
www.FormsForBook.com

If it's all sagging, you may have to put new decking on the entire roof, which is very unusual, but be prepared. Ask a roofer how much he will charge per sheet, usually around $25 - 50.

If you can, go into the attic and try to find out what is causing the sag. Perhaps it is a rotted rafter or this is where water has gotten in and the boards are rotted. You should be able to get a good idea of the extent of the damage, and then you can make an educated estimate of the cost of repairs instead of a guess.

Always require that the contractor dispose of the shingles. Otherwise, you'll be stuck with the expense. And don't pay him until he cleans the grounds to your satisfaction. Once you write that check, that ground will not get any cleaner!

### Roof Repair

Missing shingles, leaking valleys and water stains on the ceilings in the house are common repairs. Roofers will charge you according to the extent of the job, height of the job and pitch of the roof. A high job with a steep pitch will cost a lot more than a low job that the roofer can walk across. Roof repairs start at $200 and then adjust accordingly.

If the valley is leaking, the whole thing may need to be tarred or worse, re-shingled. These are costly jobs starting at $400 and could be as much as six squares if the whole thing needs to be replaced!

### Flashing

If you have a leak around the chimney, then it probably was not flashed properly or the tar around the flashing got brittle and cracked. Nonetheless, it will cost about $250 to have a chimney re-flashed and tarred.

To Get the Forms for This Book and A Free Bonus Gift visit
www.FormsForBook.com

# Flooring

### Carpet

Take a look at the carpet. Is it worn, or does it have multiple stains that will not come out? Is it outdated (avocado green, shag carpet from the 70s)? If so then you will want to replace it. If you are in doubt, replace it. People do not want to buy other people's dirt and remember, they and their kids will be walking barefoot on this carpet and they will be considering this.

To determine how much it will cost to replace carpet, you must realize that carpet is installed and sold according to the square yard. To determine the square yard you measure the length and the width of the room. Multiply these numbers and you get the total square footage of the room. Next you divided that number by nine to get the square yardage.

The best thing to do is get the measurements from all the rooms. Add all of the rooms' square feet measurements together and then divide this number by nine. This gives you the total number of yards of carpet that you are going to need.

Next, multiply that number by 1.05. This gives you a five percent fudge factor in case you screwed up the measurement of a room.

This formula can be found on the Property Inspection Worksheet, Formulas and Measurements, Flooring worksheet page.

When measuring a room, it is important that you measure from the inside of the doorway to the opposite wall, and remember to measure into closets. Do not stop at the outside of a closet because you will loose at least three feet of measurements if it is a typical closet and a lot more if it is walk-in.

To Get the Forms for This Book and A Free Bonus Gift visit
www.FormsForBook.com

Not measuring into closets or into the center of doorways is the most common flooring mistake that rehabbers make. If you do this throughout the entire house, this will add up to a lot of money quickly. I know this from experience!

Here's another thing that you have to remember: carpet is cut into 12-foot lengths. This means that one of your sides -- either length or width -- has to be equal or greater than 12 feet. For example, if you have a room that is 10 feet by eight feet, the smallest size carpet you could get is 12 feet by eight feet. Yes, you will have two feet of waste, but that is how it is done and you have to account for this in your estimate.

This comes into play when you are measuring hallways. A lot of times you will have a hallway that is eight feet by four feet, six feet by four feet, or ten feet by four feet. Each one of these measurements, for estimating purposes, should be written down as 12 feet by four feet.

If the room is 14 feet by eight feet, you are O.K. You would simply multiply the 14 by eight and divide by nine to get the amount of carpet that you will need.

As a general rule, if you have a set of stairs that has 12 steps, it takes 90 square feet of carpet to cover those steps.

Here is an example: I have a three-bedroom Colonial style house that has five rooms, a hall and a set of stairs that will need carpet. Here are the measurements:

|  | Actual Measurements | Carpet Measurements | Total Square Feet |
|---|---|---|---|
| Bedroom | 12 x 14 | 12 x 14 | 168 |
| Bedroom | 10 x 10 | *12 x 10 | 120 |
| Bedroom | 16 x 14 | 16 x 14 | 224 |
| Living room | 16 x 16 | 16 x 16 | 256 |
| Dining room | 12 x 12 | 12 x 12 | 144 |
| Hall | 6 x 4 | *12 x 12 | 144 |
| Stairs | 90 sq ft | 90 sq ft | 90 |

Total Square Footage    1,146

To Get the Forms for This Book and A Free Bonus Gift visit
www.FormsForBook.com

Divided by 9 =    128

(127.33 rounded up)

Multiplied by 1.05 =    135

(134.4 rounded up)

I'm going to need 135 yards of carpeting to complete this job.

Now that you know how much you're going to need, you've got to decide what grade of carpet you will be putting in.

Not only will you be putting in carpet, but also what is below that carpet (the pad). When you step on a nice soft carpet, it's nice and soft because it has a quality pad underneath it.

There are many grades of carpet. You do not want to get too fancy, but you do not want the absolute cheapest grade either. People can spot cheap carpet the minute they
walk into a house and will immediately be turned off. You want someone to walk through your newly rehabbed home and feel the comfort and joy that a quality carpet can give.

When choosing carpet, I recommend that you use the 28-ounce grade carpet. This is the carpet that the Federal Housing Authority allows in its buildings. It looks good; it's durable and is reasonably priced.

If I'm rehabbing an expensive house, I'll consider putting down Berber carpet. Like anything else, your repairs should match your surroundings.

Below the carpet you will be putting down the pad. Pads are quoted in pounds. The lower the pounds, the thinner the pad. You can get a four-pound, six-pound, or eight-pound pad. I recommend the six-pound pad. It's thick enough and the buyer feels (literally) that he has a quality product under his feet.

When choosing carpet, always choose a neutral color. Your tastes may not be the same as the potential buyers taste. No sense of losing a sale because they don't like the color of the carpet or worse, because the carpet does not go with their furniture.

To Get the Forms for This Book and A Free Bonus Gift visit
www.FormsForBook.com

Neutral colors go with anything. I like to use light beige. I think they call it earth tone. I've seen some rehabbers use a light gray that looks nice as well.

The installation of the carpet and pad by a contractor should cost you between $15 and $18 per yard. This is typical if you go to your local carpet dealer. You can usually get it done for less if you subcontract a carpet installer.

Most of the installers subcontract for local carpet dealers anyway. So you're basically paying the middleman fee when you go through the local dealer. Get a referral from other rehabbers in the area. Or if you happen to go by a house and see a carpet being installed, stop and ask them if they install independently, if they do, ask what they charge and take their number.

You'll want to ask them how long they have been installing for this dealer. If it's been a while, then you know that they are probably a good candidate to do subcontracting work for you. Nonetheless, ask them for the telephone numbers of people who they have done work for in the past and do your due diligence.

So using our example above, I will assume that I can have the carpet installed for $18 per yard. At $18 per yard for 135 yards, I estimate that the carpet will cost me $2,160.

### Carpet Removal
You will have to remove and dispose of the existing carpet. If you have the carpet installer do this, he will charge you approximately $3 per yard. It's usually less expensive for you to do it yourself. However, if you don't do it, do not forget about this cost.

### Carpet Cleaning
If the carpet looks to be in good condition and all that it needs is a good cleaning, then this makes me very happy because I'm going to save a lot of money. In my area the going rate for carpet cleaning is about $50 per room. In the example above with five rooms, stairs and hallway, we are looking at about $300.

To Get the Forms for This Book and A Free Bonus Gift visit
www.FormsForBook.com

Of course you can always go down to the local supermarket and rent a carpet cleaner and do it yourself. You will save money doing it this way but you won't get the professional results.

### Vinyl

You will find vinyl flooring in kitchens, bathrooms, foyers and entry ways, and sometimes in basements.

You have two options when you are replacing vinyl flooring. You can use 12-inch by 12-inch stick-on tiles or you can use sheet vinyl. The 12-inch by 12-inch stick-on tiles are something that you could possibly do yourself, but if you are going to use sheet vinyl your better off subcontracting the job out to a professional.

It's very easy to screw up a sheet vinyl job. And once screwed up, it's very hard to go back and fix.

When replacing vinyl flooring, a lot of times you will be able to go over the existing vinyl flooring. If the floor is really bad, if it's lifting on the edges, in all the seams, has holes in it or is just plain lousy, you will have to install what's called a sub-floor.

A sub-floor is a wooden floor made out of three-eighths of an inch of plywood called Leuon. At least one side of the Leuon is smooth so that you can lay the vinyl on top of it. The plywood comes in four-feet by eight-feet sheets. You calculate how many sheets you will need by taking the total square footage of the room and dividing it by 32 (which is the total square footage of a piece of Leuon).

For example, in a split-level ranch that I am currently renovating, I am replacing the sub-floor on a 14 foot by 12 foot kitchen. I multiply 14 by 12 and this gives me a total square footage of 168. Divide the 168 by 32 and I will need 5.25 sheets to complete the job. I always round up, so I would buy six sheets.

When installing a sub-floor, it must be nailed down properly. The nails you will need to use are called ring nails. They have rings going up the shaft to prevent the nail from lifting and thus keep the sub-floor secure.

To Get the Forms for This Book and A Free Bonus Gift visit
www.FormsForBook.com

You nail each seam (where the boards meet or where the board meets a wall or cabinet) with a nail approximately one-half inch in from the seam and insert a nail every six inches.

When nailing the interior of the board, you stagger the nails every 10 inches across and down. So if you start your first nail 10 inches in going across and two inches down from the top. And then every nail going down should be about 10 inches apart.

The next nail going across should be nailed seven inches down. This will be half of the distance between the first nail ( 2 + 5 = 7). And then nail every 10 inches going down.

Alternate between two inches down and seven inches down going across the board. This will give you a staggered pattern. This is what you want. You do not want perfect rows. This allows the sub-floor to stay secure to the floor.

Of course you will have to cut some of the Leuon pieces to fit the floor. You do this with a skill saw but remember to use the right blade. If you use a ripping blade you will rip this very thin plywood to shreds. If you don't have a Lueon blade then take you're ripping blade off and put it on backwards. This works very well.

After you have nailed every nail down, you must then examine the sub floor and make sure that no nail head is sticking up. If a nail head is sticking up from the floor, even the slightest bit, that nail head will tear through your vinyl. Maybe not the first day, but shortly thereafter. And all the hard work will be for nothing.

After you have checked for raised nail heads, get a floor-leveling agent. You can get this at any hardware store. You will need this mix and a trowel. Mix up the leveling agent and level off every nail head, because now each one should have an indentation into the sub-floor and you want to bring the area back up to level. This is time consuming but worth it.

When you are done leveling each hole, let it dry overnight and then lightly sand each one. Give the floor a good sweeping and you're ready to install your vinyl.

If you are going to hire a subcontractor to install the sub-floor, they usually charge per sheet. In my area, it is approximately $23 per sheet. If you use this figure your estimate should be close.

Should you use stick-on tiles or sheet vinyl? Simple rule to follow: If you are doing it yourself, use stick-on; if you are going to subcontract out, use sheet vinyl. I happen to think that sheet vinyl looks better, but I started out installing all of my own floors with stick-ons and didn't have any problem selling those houses.

Here's the rule when using sheet vinyl: Use a medium grade. Armstrong puts out a good medium grade sheet vinyl. You can request whatever you want from the subcontractor who is going to put down the floor. If he has a comparable product that he can get cheaper for you, by all means use it. Make sure that it is at least the medium grade of thickness.

If it's any thinner, the floor will tear very easily. So easily, in fact, that I have had a woman's high heal shoe tear my floors on more than one occasion before I smartened up and used a better grade floor.

Figuring out how much a floor will cost is the same as with carpet. Figure out the total number of yards and multiply by the cost. Good sheet vinyl should be installed for about $17 to $28 per yard. If you are using a sub-floor, don't forget to add this cost in. (You won't forget if you follow my list!)

If you have small rooms, such as a small kitchen and a small bathroom, a subcontractor may charge you a minimum charge (the lowest amount of money that he would be willing to do the job for) that may be higher than the cost when calculating the total yardage.

What I do, if the total cost for the vinyl comes out less than $750 and I'm going to subcontract it, I use $750 as my estimate cost.

If you are going to do it yourself and use stick on tiles, here are a couple of general rules of thumb. Always start in the middle of the room, not at one side. If you center a tile in the middle of the room you should have approximately one half a tile to cut on each wall to complete the floor.

If you start on one wall and work across the room, you may end up with just a sliver of tile needed to complete the job on the other side, it will cost you more money for the tiles, and it is a hassle to make those small cuts to get that last piece to fit.

Make sure you start with a clean floor. If you do not need a sub-floor, the first thing you will have to do is fill in any cracks or seams from the previous floor with the floor level. If the previous floor was a 12-inch by 12-inch tile floor, you will need to fill in all of those seams with the floor level. If there are any lifting sections, either on the sides or in the middle, simply cut those lifting sections off so that it is nice and secure and use the floor-leveling agent to bring the floor level to the existing floor. Then let it dry and lightly sand it.

Again, make sure that your floor is clean! Any minute piece of dirt, pebble or dried floor level will show up under your new floor after you install it. What I do is keep a hand broom and a rag with me. Each time I go to install a new tile, I give the new 12-inch by 12-inch area a quick sweep and a wipe. This almost guarantees a perfect floor.

How much does it cost to lay down a 12-inch by 12-inch floor? Usually a lot less than what it would cost to have sheet vinyl installed. You can pick up a good box of tile for about $22 a box. Be careful when you choose a tile. Make sure that you are getting the most tiles for your money. Some boxes are sold with 45 tiles in a box and some are sold with less. When comparing prices, make sure you are getting what you paid for.

If one box is $22 and you get 45 tiles, and the other is $14 but you only get 28 tiles, the $22 tile box is the better deal!

Calculate how many boxes you will need and how much floor prep is needed and you can determine how much to estimate for your stick-on floor. It should cost you about a third of what a sheet vinyl floor would cost, especially if you are doing it yourself.

When choosing vinyl flooring, stick with neutral colors. You won't be living in the house so don't choose what you would like. Your tastes are different, so are mine. A nice beige floor is what I always use.

Do not choose all white. I have had women walk through some of my houses that have had white floors and shriek! They say that they will never be able to keep it clean. Choose a floor that is neutral in color but will hide the dirt. If you don't know what I mean, ask anyone who has had to keep a floor clean.

One other consideration, if you have a tile floor that is beyond repair and you need to remove it to put down some vinyl, you will need a sub-floor.

### Tile
I will not install tile over a linoleum floor unless it is a very rare case when the house would warrant it to match its surroundings. This would usually be an expensive house in an expensive neighborhood.

If the house already had tile floors in need of repairs, the first thing I will do is to attempt to match the tile. Usually the tile is no longer being made and can't be matched. If it can't be matched, then I have the option of leaving it or removing it and replacing it with either new tile or vinyl.

If it can be matched then I replace the broken tiles. When doing this, bring a piece of the grout (the material between the tiles) into the tile store so that it can be matched as well. Grout comes in all colors.

If it is just cracked in one or two tiles and the floor still looks good, I keep it. Sometimes the tiles are O.K. but the color and style are from a different era. Such as the 1950's art deco style pink bathrooms or the 1970's avocado green or harvest gold. These tiles date the house and I always remove them.

If the tile needs to be taken up I almost always replace with vinyl, unless the house itself warrants new tile.

When replacing a tile floor with vinyl, you need a sub-floor so include it in your estimate.

When replacing a tile floor with tile, a tile subcontractor will charge you $4 to $6 per square foot to install. **You must supply the tile.** Tile can be cheap or expensive. You can get good inexpensive tile at Home Depot or Lowe's or any of the big box do-it-yourself stores. I usually pick it up for $2 to $3 per tile. A 12-foot by 12-foot kitchen can easily cost you $1,300 (144 square feet, $6 to install, $3 per tile, 9 x 144 = 1300).

As you can see, this costs much more. You almost always need a sub-contractor to install it because you need a special wet saw to cut the tile and it takes a lot of skill.

**Hardwood Floors**

Unless you have some experience refinishing hardwood floors, I suggest that you hire a subcontractor. One small stall as you are sanding the floors leaves a little groove. Do this throughout the floor, and you have a lot of unsightly grooves. I tried refinishing floors twice before I got smart and started subbing it out. The pros make them come out looking like glass. There is nothing more impressive in a home than gleaming hardwood floors.

If you have a house where they covered the hardwood floors with carpet, remove the carpet and refinish the floors. If the carpets are good, save them for another house.

Prices for hardwood floor subcontractors are:
.75 cents to $1.10 per square foot
$10 to $20 per stair tread
$20 to $30 per closet

You will have the option to use water-based polyurethane. This finish is more durable and long lasting, but I would only use it if I were going to do the floors in my own house.

To Get the Forms for This Book and A Free Bonus Gift visit
www.FormsForBook.com

The regular polyurethane finish that is normally used is just fine. As matter of fact it's better than fine, it looks great!

Here's an example: I recently rehabbed a house that had six rooms of hardwood flooring. Two of the three bedrooms were hardwood. Would I consider installing hardwood in the third bedroom? Usually not. It costs a lot less to replace the carpet than to install a new hardwood floor. The stairs going up to the second floor were also hardwood. This is how I priced it:

Assume .90 cents per square foot, $15 for stair treads and $25 for closets.

|  | L x W | Total Square Feet |
|---|---|---|
| Family Room | 14 x 14 | 196 |
| Living Room | 14 x 12 | 168 |
| Dining Room | 12 x 12 | 144 |
| Bedroom | 10 x 10 | 100 |
| Bedroom | 16 x 14 | 224 |
|  | Total | 832 |

Each bedroom has a closet, and there is one closet in the living room.

There are 14 total stair treads on the stairs.

| | | | | | |
|---|---|---|---|---|---|
| Total square footage | 832 | x | 00.90 | = | 748.00 |
| Total closets | 3 | x | 25.00 | = | 75.00 |
| Total stair treads | 14 | x | 15.00 | = | 60.00 |
| | | | Total cost of Hardwood Floors | | $ 884.00 |

Notice that when I calculated the square footage for the hardwood floors, I didn't increase the 10 foot by 10 foot room to a 12 foot by 10 foot. This is because we only do this with carpet. Also notice that I was calculating total square feet and not square yards, so I did not divide the square footage by nine as I did when calculating for carpeting.

To Get the Forms for This Book and A Free Bonus Gift visit
www.FormsForBook.com

### Hardwood Floor Repair

Repairs vary, depending on the size of the repair (replacing a couple of rotted boards below a radiator is about the average size of a repair). Repairs usually start at $125 and go up.

# Structural

When you are walking through a house and you notice that the floor is sagging to the left or to the right, you probably have a structural problem. Something in the basement is not right. It could be a rotted beam (horizontal support), lally column (vertical support), sill (the last piece of wood between the walls and the foundation on the exterior walls), a combination of the three or all three. I have seen all three in the same house before.

The most common causes of rot are two things -- water and insects. Water because either the yard was not graded properly or the gutters are not relieving the water away from the house, and insects because they like to eat wood.

Always consult with a contractor and get a bid before you attempt to purchase a house with structural problems. It takes experience to be able to determine the extent of the damage that these elements create. Most of the time they can be fixed and a lot of people are afraid of houses with structural problems, so this is a good and very profitable niche market.

### Engineering Inspection

If it is really bad, you may elect to have an structural engineering inspection done or the local building inspector may require that you have a structural engineer look at the problem and give a full report. These reports can cost from $250 to $800.

Bring this report to the building inspector and ask him what he wants done. This is critical. If what you think needs to be done is different from what the building inspector thinks needs to be done, he wins every time, and you have usually underestimated the repairs. I did, too, before I smartened up!

To Get the Forms for This Book and A Free Bonus Gift visit
www.FormsForBook.com

Do a visual inspection of all the floors in the house. Look at the doorways. If the house is out of kilter, it always shows in the upper frame of the doorway. Of course, most houses settle over time, especially the older ones, so if they are a little crooked, this may be normal. If they are very crooked, it's time to hire a professional.

In the basement, do a visual inspection of the floor joist, beams, lally columns and sills. If you see pock marks or a white powder on the surface of any of these wood surfaces, you either have insects or had them. Now you have to determine two things: Are they still active, and how much damage did they do? You'll have to have a professional pest inspection to determine if they are still active. If they are, they will have to be treated. Insect treatment can run from $300 for a small area of powder post beetles or up to $1,800 for a full termite treatment.

To determine the extent of the damage, take a screwdriver and jam it into the wood. If the screwdriver inserts more than a quarter of an inch into the wood, it may have to be replaced. If it goes further, it definitely needs to be replaced. You can replace small sections or large ones, it all depends on the extent of the damage. Get an estimate, though this screwdriver test should give you an idea of what you're in for.

One of the biggest problems with houses with no basements is that the termites go directly from the ground into the walls. Before you know it, half of your wall has been eaten out. When buying these houses, you should always have a pest inspection.  A pest inspection cost about $150, but it is well worth it. Think of it as an inexpensive insurance policy.

### Grading
Take a look at the grounds. If they slope towards the house instead of away from it, you're going to have a water problem, if the house doesn't already have one. It's easy to fix, just add dirt until it slopes the other way. Of course if the house is at the bottom of a hill, you may have a problem. You may then elect to install a French Drain.

### French Drain
To make a French Drain, dig a hole around the exterior of the house ( these can also be done in the basement) about three to four feet

deep. This kind of looks like a moat in the beginning stages. A PVC (plastic) pipe is then laid at the bottom of the moat. The PVC has holes in it to allow water to penetrate it. It is then covered with rocks up to ground level. The very top is covered with a layer of soil.

Before the water can come in contact with the house, it falls through the layer of soil, through the very porous rocks and into the PVC drain pipe. The pipe is graded so that all the water is directed away from the house into a safe area somewhere in the yard.

If the French Drain is in the cellar, the water is directed to a sump pump which then pumps the water out of the house.

French Drains can be expensive -- anywhere from $5,000 to $15,000 and up. Get an estimate.

### Cracked Foundation
A lot of times foundations crack due to settling. This is usually not a problem unless water enters the basement when it rains. Nobody wants a house if the basement gets water. They are hard to sell. Cracks are easy to fix with sealants, though sometimes in slab houses the problem is so bad that the floor has to be re-poured in a certain area.

Many old houses in the northern states have fieldstone foundations. And through the years the parge that held the fieldstones together (kind of like a cement) wears away and water seeps in through the openings. You can do a couple of things with this problem. The first is to re-parge the area to seal the leaks. Get a dry parging mix, add the necessary water and fill in where needed. Sometimes there are many small leaks. They now sell a special sealant paint for basements that you can paint over the walls and floors and it seals up all the leaks. It works pretty well.

### Masonry
A lot of houses with brick entry steps have a brick or two loose on the corners of the steps. Remove the bricks, chisel off any dried mortar on the brick or on the surface area, reapply fresh mortar, press the brick(s) back into place and scrape away any excess mortar matching the pattern of the surrounding joints. I usually estimate this repair at $100 if it's a couple of bricks. If it is a whole row, I increase accordingly.

To Get the Forms for This Book and A Free Bonus Gift visit
www.FormsForBook.com

While we are on the subject of the masonry front steps, a lot of masonry steps come with iron hand rails imbedded into them. If they are worn looking and in need of paint then I scrape them with a wire brush and spray them with a high gloss enamel spray paint, the kind that comes in a can. Be sure to tape newspaper to the house and the brick work so that the paint does not get on those surfaces. This is a quick job usually no more than two hours of work. Figure in about $75 dollars to your estimate.

If bricks are broken or missing then you will have to replace them. This is a little more costly. The handrail itself costs about $175. If you need both sides, double the price. To install these handrails, one side is usually attached to the house while the other is imbedded into the masonry steps. You will have to drill out the old anchor, this is where it is usually broken off, create a new cavity, insert the end of handrail and fill with mortar, scraping away any excess.

Here's a tip when working with mortar. After you have scraped away the excess mortar when installing bricks or handrails, immediately clean off the area with water. Either spray it with a hose or brush it down because the mortar has left a very fine film that you cannot see right now but when it dries it will cover your nice red brick with a gray mortar color. After it dries you cannot get it off.

Always look at the chimneys on the roof. A lot of times the mortar will have weathered away between the bricks. The chimney will then need to be "re-pointed." Depending upon the size of the chimney, its height and pitch to the roof, the average re-pointing job will cost $250 to $350.

Also check the chimney in the cellar; this too may need some re-pointing. If you don't see it the home inspector for the buyer will. The average cost to re-point a basement chimney is $150.

If you have concrete steps that have edges that are broken off or a surface that is worn away, it will need to be patched using cement. For a worn away surface, such as a hole, clean the area removing any loose debris and then brush the area with concrete bonding adhesive. Next, fill and smooth the hole with a trowel. Let dry.

To Get the Forms for This Book and A Free Bonus Gift visit
www.FormsForBook.com

When repairing worn away edges on treads you need to build a form. The easiest way to do this is to cut a board the height of the step riser, press if flush with the riser and brace it into position using heavy blocks making sure that the top of the form is level with the top of the tread. Apply the concrete bonding adhesive to the cleaned area and using a trowel, press a stiff mixture of quick-setting cement into the damaged area. Use a wood float to smooth the surface of the cement area. You will need to round off the front edge of the step with an edger and use a trowel for the side.

Again, depending upon the size of the repair, the average concrete step repair will cost $100 to $170.

# Exterior

### Landscaping
Always put quality landscaping in front of your house. If it is old and overgrown, pull it out and add new shrubs, bushes and flowers. Take a picture of the house and bring it to your local nursery. They will give you a nice design to make your house look more attractive. I usually put $500 to $1500 as a landscaping allowance.

Mailbox and house numbers should match and look good. I like to use gold mailboxes and house numbers if possible. It gives my house a little extra curb appeal, which I'll get deeper into in another chapter. One hundred dollars will get you a quality mailbox and numbers.

# Miscellaneous Monsters!

### Oil Tanks
Never, never, never, never buy a house with an underground oil tank. Always have it removed first, even if it's a great deal and the owner says take it or leave it, if he is not removing the tank….leave it. The risk is too great.

To Get the Forms for This Book and A Free Bonus Gift visit
www.FormsForBook.com

If that tank had developed a hole in it at any time in the last 20 years that it has been in the ground and oil has leaked out of it, you will be responsible for the cleanup. The Environmental Protection Agency will go after the owner of record, which will be you. Even if the property is in a trust, you are not protected.

The amount of oil that has leaked into the ground will determine the amount of the clean up. The starting price is about $4,800 and can go to up well over $100,000.

Unfortunately, I know this from experience. I bought a house where there was no indication of an underground oil tank. There was an oil tank in the basement feeding the existing furnace that looked like it had been there for years. The owner was asked among other things if there were any underground oil tanks, and she said no. I had a home inspection prior to the purchase, and again, no disclosure of a tank.

Six weeks into the job I get a call from my foreman, who says that on the far side of the house, in the bushes, there is a pipe sticking up out of the ground that looks like an underground oil tank.

I wasn't happy but I'm not a pessimist and I was more upset at the fact the it was going to cost me $1,200 that I wasn't counting on spending to get it out. That's the normal rate to remove a clean tank from the ground.

When the tank removal specialist dug down to the tank he found two holes in the tank the size of half dollars more than halfway down the side of the tank. This was not good news. There had been an obvious oil leak. How extensive was yet to be determined. Every time a tank is dug out, you must pull a permit, and a representative from the fire department is there to make sure that the tank is whole. If it isn't, soil samples are taken to find the extent of the spill.

So now I know I'm looking at least $4,800, and this makes me even more unhappy. To make a long story short, one year and four months later the job was completed. It turned out that the tank had been leaking for years. The oil got into the water table and saturated the entire yard. They had to dig 11 feet below the cellar floor to get all of the saturated oil out of from under the house. They dug, tested and hauled away contaminated soil for almost a year and four months. The final bill came out to be $157,000! As of now, I am still chasing the previous owner and her insurance company to try to collect something, anything, from this mess!

I could have done one thing to prevent this from happening. I could have checked with the local fire department to see if there were any underground tanks in that yard. The fire department has all the records pertaining to underground tanks. Of course I always do it now, but if I had done it then, I would have a few more hairs in my head and a lot more money in my bank account! Had this happened when I first started out, I would not be in this game today.

### Septic Systems

Always have the septic system pumped, inspected and tested. Some states have a strict septic system compliance program. If you have a bad system, the replacement will start at $4,000 for inspection, certified plans by the engineer, installation by the contractor and as built plans by the certified engineer after the job is complete. A new system can be as high as $50,000. Very unusual, but it can get that high. I know of a $46,000 septic system installation by one of the rehabbers in my area. Cover your butt and make sure you have a good system before you take over the property.

Don't buy a house that you cannot inspect, especially if the owner says that he knows that the septic system is not good but he's not going to replace it. At least have the owner do the engineering so that you can get estimates. Otherwise you're playing Russian roulette. You're an investor, not a gambler.

### Lead Paint

States are getting tougher and tougher on houses that have lead paint. If you're buying apartment buildings, you do not want to have lead paint in your building if you have more than one bedroom. Otherwise you risk a child under six becoming poisoned by the lead in the paint. If this happens you will have a dreaded lead paint law suit, for which you will

To Get the Forms for This Book and A Free Bonus Gift visit
www.FormsForBook.com

not be covered by your insurance company. Insurance companies stopped insuring lead paint a few years ago.

Although states are getting tougher on the issue of lead paint, they are becoming a little more lenient as to how you can remedy the situation. Some states allow the owner to paint over the lead with a special paint. This is called encapsulation, and is the least expensive method.

Others require that you strip or remove the lead paint off any surface that is palatable (that can be eaten by a child) below five feet and the first six inches of any corner. If you opt to have the paint stripped, you will need to hire a contractor who will secure the area with plastic so that none of the lead paint dust gets into the air.

Children are poisoned more by inhaling the dust of lead paint than they are from actually chewing on the paint chips. The reason that they chew on the chips is that the lead in the paint actually taste sweet. Most of the dust that is inhaled comes from the windows. From opening and closing the windows, the abrasion creates dust, the dust settles on the window sill and when it is opened and a breeze comes in, it is blown into the room.

Some states are now allowing owners to remove and replace the contaminated wood themselves, thus saving them lots of money in contracting fees.

If you are going to hire a lead paint contractor to abate the lead, typical costs run from $4,000 to $9,000 a unit. One of the biggest expenses is the window replacement. In older homes, the windows are usually contaminated with lead paint, if not on the inside then on the exterior of the sash. It is not cost effective to scrape the windows to bare wood, they usually must be replaced.

On the following page you will find the Wealthy Investors Quick Guide Secrets to Rehab Costs. Although it is not as thorough as the material that we have just gone over, you can use the guide as a quick cheat sheet when you are at a property or an auction and are trying to get an idea if the deal is going to make any sense.

If it looks like the deal is going to make sense, then go back and do all the long form calculations to make sure your estimations are as close as possible.

# Quick Guide To Rehab Costs

| | |
|---|---|
| *Clean Outs* | $400 to $500 per dumpster, $25 per man hour |
| *Sheetrock* | $75 per fist size hole, $4 per square foot for large areas |
| *Interior Paint* | $1,500 for an average three bedroom house |
| *Exterior Paint* | $3,500 for an average one level three bedroom house |
| *Interior Door* | Leuon, Masonite $75 door only$130 pre-hung |
| | Solid core Leuon $100 per door |
| | Wood $150 per door |
| *Exterior Door* | Metal pre-hung, three lights $250 |
| | Storm Door $150 |
| *Interior Trim* | $3 to $5 per linear foot |
| *Exterior Trim* | Average repair $150 |
| *Cabinets* | $25 to $40 per cabinet installed |
| *Vanity/Sink Combo* | $250 installed |
| *Counters* | $750 standard not custom |
| *Garage Doors* | $800 regular size, $1,100 oversized |
| *Fencing* | $45 per section |
| *Vinyl Siding* | $5,500 average one level three bedroom house |
| *Windows* | $175 installed (vinyl clad) |
| *Gutters* | $5 per linear foot, metal |
| *Electrical* | Panel upgrade $1,200 |
| | Full service upgrade $3,500 |
| *Furnace* | Hot air $2,500 |
| | Forced hot water $3,300 |
| *Condenser* | $1,750 |

To Get the Forms for This Book and A Free Bonus Gift visit
www.FormsForBook.com

| | | |
|---|---|---|
| ***Tub*** | Install new | $900 |
| ***Symons Valve*** | $165 | |
| ***Sink*** | $150 installed | |
| ***Faucets*** | . $150 (get nice ones) | |
| ***Appliances*** | Stove | $450 |
| | Dishwater | $425 |
| | Disposal | $120 |
| | Refrigerator | $600 |
| ***Roofing*** | Overlay | $200 per square |
| | Strip | $275 per square |
| ***Carpet*** | $150 per room | |
| ***Vinyl*** | $750 allowance | |
| ***Landscaping*** | $750 allowance | |

# *Chapter 9*

# "Order Of Repairs"

You'll want to spend some time planning who is going to do what and when. An efficiently planned job will save you time, and most importantly, money! Some repairs cannot (and some should not) be done before others. For instance, you do not want to have the floors refinished or the carpet installed until last, because you risk them being damaged by contractors carelessly walking over them to perform other tasks.

Sometimes walls cannot be repaired and prepped for painting until the electrician is done with his work, because there is the possibility that the electrician will need to make additional holes in the walls to snake wires.

The painting should not be done until the walls are completely repaired. No painting should be started until all the repairs have been sanded. If you start painting too early (while other walls are being sanded), the compound dust gets into the air and onto your freshly painted walls, sticking to the walls and making them look bad.

New outlet covers should not be installed until the painting has been completed so that no one paints over them.

New landscaping should not be done until the roof has been stripped (dropping shingles will ruin the new plants).

I have created the Rehab Planning Schedule so that you can have a bird's eye view of the entire rehab. With a quick look you can plan what needs to be done when, who needs to be on the site, and who should be ready to come on right after them.

Here is a list of what repairs should be done, and in what order:

**Exterior**
Clean out yard of debris
Repair trim work
Roof
Repair/replace any decking
Window replacement
Siding
Painting
Gutters
Masonry work
Landscaping

Here's the logic behind it. You first clean out the yard of debris and mow the lawn to start off with a clean work area. You may think, "Well, it's just going to be made a mess anyway, why don't we clean it after?" Wrong. If you start with a messy work area, it will just keep getting messier and messier, and before you know it you have the neighbors backing up their trucks to dump off their trash. Why not, the place looks like a dump, so it must be a dump.

Next, the local Board of Health will come down and issue a clean-up order. Then they will go back to City Hall and tell everyone else in the inspectional services what a mess the house is and what a careless person the owner is. Since they now consider the owner to be careless and irresponsible, they will pay special attention to your property and make sure that you meet every letter of the law, which usually costs you more money in the long run. Do yourself a favor, demand that your contractors pick up after themselves at the end of every day. Go so far as to fine them for a messy worksite.

The trim work will be the first job that will need to be completed. To be precise, you will need to replace any rotted soffit and facia before the roof work begins because the roofer will be attaching a thin metal strip on the bottom edges of the roof. This metal strip is appropriately called edging. It helps prevent water from penetrating the roof decking thus

To Get the Forms for This Book and A Free Bonus Gift visit
www.FormsForBook.com

preventing rot. The remainder of the trim can be done at this time or after the roof work is done. Usually your roofer will replace the rotted trim boards, so ask him to price it into the job, but ask him to itemize it so that you can see what he will be charging you for this part of the job.

Your roofer should be ready to be on the job the day after the closing. This means that while the contract has been pending, you have gotten your bids, chosen your roofer and scheduled his crew to be on your site for a specific date. Everyone is busy and needs to be scheduled well in advance.

Once the soffits and fascias have been repaired, the roof work is done first to prevent any water from getting into the house and ruining the work that has already been done. Even if the roof is not leaking now, when the work is being completed, there is a chance that it may rain while the contractor is in the middle of the repairs. If he doesn't tarp the roof off properly or if there is really heavy wind and that tarp is blown off, you're in trouble.

Never install gutters before the roof is done. The ladders that your contractor uses to get on the roof will dent and damage your new gutters. When a roofer strips a roof, he simply scrapes off the old shingles with a specially designed shovel. He scrapes and lets the shingles cascade down the roof and over the edge. Stripped shingles will accumulate in the gutters, clogging them and sometimes over-weighting them to the point where they bend. If they get into the downspouts, you'll have to remove them to get the shingles out. Then you will have to reinstall them.

Falling shingles have been known to ruin a good paint job or leave black marks on the vinyl siding. And if you install your new plants and shrubs before you do the roof, between the workmen moving the ladders and the falling shingles, you may need to replant after the roof is done.

If you are having your roof stripped, make sure your roofer puts a tarp that is attached to the edge of the roof (or better yet, the facia board), and that it is long enough to cover your landscaping and reach the ground. This tarp will protect the landscaping that is currently in place.

Make sure your contract calls for the roofer to clean up after himself every day and that it is his responsibility to haul off his debris. Do not pay the roofer in full until the yard is as clean as you want it. Otherwise, you will be cleaning it.

As the roof work is being finished, finish off any trim work. Repair and replace any decking (porches) work that needs to be done and do any siding repair. While you're doing the brunt of the carpentry work, you can also be replacing the windows.

The windows should be ordered just before closing. You can have the manufacturers rep out to measure the windows, but don't submit the order until you are sure that the deal is going to close. If you don't close and the windows have been made to order, you will have to pay for them. This is an expensive lesson. Windows take about seven to 10 days to be delivered onto the site. I try to get my order in five days prior to closing.

Windows can be installed at the same time as the roofers are working. Multi-tasking jobs are the way you will save time and money. So, prior to the closing, you have chosen the contractor you want to install your windows. You and he have scheduled the day that he is to start. This means that you must have those windows on order and ready to go at the appropriate time.

Now you're ready to work with the siding of the house. If you had to remove cedar shingles, this work could be done while the roofers are working. And if you are reinstalling cedar shingles, this can also be done while the roofers are doing their job. There is very little chance of damage to cedar shingles from roofing work.

If you're painting, all the siding repair, trim work and decking work will have been completed before you start to paint. Your painters can, however, begin scraping and priming while this is being done. Landscaping is not done prior to the painting for the same reason that it is not done prior to the roofing. Paint chips, splatters and ladders will ruin your new landscaping.

Make sure your painters tarp off the existing landscaping and below their ladders as they work there way around the house. There is nothing worse than seeing trees and shrubs with paint splatters all over them and if that paint splatters onto your concrete foundation it's very difficult to get off. Also, paint chips all over a yard are unsightly and if the paint contains lead, you may have created an environmental issue.

If you are vinyl siding the house, your contractor should be ready to roll at this point. You've gotten an estimate from the roofer about how long it's going to take him to finish his job. You've given an allowance for bad weather, since roofers don't work in the rain. I usually figure in a day lost due to weather on the roofer's schedule, so I schedule my siding contractor accordingly. When the roofer is done with at least one side of the house, I want my siding contractor to begin working on that side thus saving me time, and in the long run, money.

You must have the new windows installed on the side of the house that is being vinyl sided prior to it being vinyl sided. This is because the new windows have to be trimmed with "J" channel as they vinyl side it. This is much harder to do after the fact.

Now you've got either the painting complete or the vinyl siding done. The soffits and facias are repaired, painted, or wrapped in siding. Now you can install the gutters. The gutters are attached to the facia boards; This is why they are done when all of the previous work has been completed.

Next you can perform any landscaping and masonry work that needs to be completed, and now you have a great looking house on the exterior.

While you have crews completing the exterior work, you will also have crews working on the inside of the house as well. Below is the order in which interior repairs are usually made.

**Interior**
Clean out debris in house
Toilet repair
Removal of any flooring
Plumbing repair/replace
Electrical repair/replace

To Get the Forms for This Book and A Free Bonus Gift visit
www.FormsForBook.com

Replace/repair windows
Remove wallpaper
Repair walls and trim
Repair/replace doors
Repair ceilings
Install cabinets
Install counters
Install sinks
Install faucets
Paint interior
Install new lighting
Install new switch plate and outlet covers
Install flooring
Install appliances

The start of the interior repairs begins with the clean out. Have your clean out crew in the house the day after the closing. This starts everyone off with a nice clean work area. Insist that all of your contractors and crews clean up after themselves nightly. You never know when a potential buyer may come strolling through the property.

The first thing you will want to do is have a working toilet. Everyone needs to use it during the day, and without one you're going to lose a lot of man hours running to the nearest gas station. Put tissue paper in the bathroom. If you don't, they will use anything, and I mean anything! This usually results with a clog in the toilet that will need to be snaked out (an unnecessary additional cost).

Have your plumbers and electricians ready to begin the day after closing, which means you have gotten the bids and scheduled them. Waiting until you close before you get your bids and commitments from these contractors will cost you a lot of time and is a very common mistake that people make.

Plumbers and electricians sometimes have to open walls or tear up floors. You want them in first, not only to get the systems up and running, but also to see the extent of the damage that their repairs are going to cause you.

To Get the Forms for This Book and A Free Bonus Gift visit
www.FormsForBook.com

If you wait to have this work done, you will end up redoing repairs that had been completed.

While the plumbers and electricians are doing their thing, you can have other crews doing a number of other things. If you have any wallpaper to be removed, now is the time to do it. This will allow you to see if any walls need to be repaired below the wallpaper, and you will be ready to prep the walls for painting.

Window replacement should be going on at this time. Walls and trim, doors and ceilings can all be worked on simultaneously. You may have a lot of people working on your house at the same time. It may look confusing, but smile because this is just what you want. As long as it is done in the proper order, you are maximizing your time with multi-tasking and getting your job done efficiently. It is always a joy to walk on to a job site and hear the sounds of happy hammers!

Cabinetry work is started next. The old kitchen should have been removed with the clean out. The new kitchen cabinets are brought in and ready to be installed. After your cabinets are installed in both the kitchen and the bath, you can install the countertops.

Here's a tip! Cover the newly installed countertops with the cardboard boxes that the cabinets came in. This will protect them from the numerous things that will accumulate on top of them as the different contractors complete their work. All it takes is a couple of power tools to be hastily placed on your new countertops to scratch, dent or chip them. If you don't cover them, this **will** happen, **guaranteed**.

Next, install the kitchen sink and faucet. If you have an existing garbage disposal or are installing a new one, now is the time to do it. Instruct the painting contractor not to clean his brushes in that sink. This is the fastest way to ruin a garbage disposal.

You should instruct the painting contractor to clean his brushes using an outside faucet, making sure that he cleans the ground around it each time. If it is winter and he must clean his brushes inside, then have him use the bathroom sink and tell him to run the hot water for a while after his clean up to prevent paint building up in the trap (part of the drain). Most painters know this, but don't assume anything. If the sink clogs from paint, make it the painter's responsibility that it be repaired.

After, and only after, all of the previous work has been completed, then you begin the preparations for the painting. All the walls should be smooth, outlet covers and switch plates should all be removed, lights should be hanging from the ceiling so that the painters can paint below the base, and floors should be tarped off properly.

After the interior of the house has been painted, it is now time to install the flooring. Install all carpeting, lino, tile and/or refinish the floors at this time. Here are some tips to remember.

You should remove the toilet and vanity when you install tile and/or lino in the bathroom. This gives a more professional looking finish.

However, you don't need to install the flooring before you install your kitchen cabinets.

After the hardwood floors are refinished, expect to do touch-up painting on the baseboards. The sanding machines bang the heck out of them and leave a lot of scrape marks.

Extra strips of carpet are called remnants. Lay the remnants over the new rug and tile in the most commonly used paths (by the doorways, hallways and walkways). This will protect the carpet and tile while it is being shown to potential buyers.

As the flooring is completed, you should also be installing all of the new lighting, switch plate and outlet covers, and any other touch-up finish work that needs to be done.

Now install the appliances and you are done. Congratulations! You have just completed your rehab. Now let's get that house sold!!

# Planning Repairs
# Quick Guide

Exterior:

1. Clean out yard of debris
2. Repair trim work
3. Roof
4. Repair/replace any decking
5. Window replacement
6. Siding
7. Painting
8. Gutters
9. Masonry work
10. Landscaping

Interior:

1. Clean out of debris in house
2. Toilet repair
3. Removal of any flooring
4. Plumbing repair/replace
5. Electrical repair/replace
6. Replace/repair windows
7. Remove wallpaper
8. Repair walls and trim
9. Repair/replace door
10. Repair ceilings
11. Install cabinets
12. Install counters
13. Install sinks
14. Install faucets
15. Paint interior
16. Install new lighting
17. Install new switch plate and outlet covers
18. Install flooring
19. Install appliances

# Chapter 10
## Repairs That Will Make You The Most Money

The most important things that every new homeowner is looking for are convenience, cleanliness and security.

Simply put, kitchens and bathrooms sell houses. Why? Because this is where the family spends most of its time and more importantly, this is where the homemaker of the house spends most of his or her time while taking care of the family.

A clean, bright, modern kitchen and bath will do more to sell your house than anything else. This being the case, you want your kitchen to look as big as possible. If changing the cabinets, use light wood or even white cabinets. When installing new flooring, use a light neutral color, and match it with a light color on the walls along with the trim, which is painted a clean looking semi-gloss white.

The cabinets may be O.K., but if you changed that hardware you might really sharpen them up! Perhaps in the sink you may put one of those fancy drain covers, because you don't see too many of those and for $5 you can really make an impression.

If the appliances look worn at all, replace them. Spend a little extra on a sharp looking stove and make sure it is self-cleaning. A dishwasher can be a make or break item. If you don't have a dishwasher in the house, you may lose the sale for that reason alone. Who wants to spend all of their time doing dishes?

The bathrooms should be neat and clean. Do any grouting and caulking work that needs to be done in the tub/shower area. No one wants to clean themselves in someone else's dirt. If the tub can be refinished, do it.

Install a fancy shower curtain and towel rack.

The fixtures (tub/shower, toilet, sink) should match (if possible) and they should be in modern colors. The sink should have a fancy faucet. The medicine cabinet or mirror, the item that they will be looking into everyday of their lives, should be visually appealing.

In the closets throughout the house, you may consider installing closet organizers. Women love these.

Take a look at the roof. Is it in good condition? If it's not, the potential buyer is going to start to get nervous fast. In their minds, a new roof is big money. Even if it's only an eight square low pitch roof that would cost $2,500 to replace, this is the fastest way to lose a new buyer.

Psychologically, when a buyer sees a bad roof as he pulls up to the property, no matter how nice the rest of the house looks, in his mind he is wondering what else is wrong that he can't see.

Don't make the mistake of having the mentality that if the home inspector says that the roof needs to be replaced, and **then** you will replace it because maybe you can get away with it. The only thing that is going to get away is your prospective buyer. Many buyers will not even give you an offer based on how a roof looks. Some buyers don't know how to negotiate, or worse, they are afraid to negotiate, and the only person who will lose is you. Besides, chances are you're going to have to replace that bad looking roof anyway. Do it while you're doing the rest of the repairs. It should already be factored into your estimate.

The heating system should be cleaned and look shiny, even if it is an older model. A good cleaning can go a long way toward making a new homeowner feel secure. It is a good idea to have it serviced, and have an inspection tag from the plumber hanging from the pipe stating when it was inspected and that everything is in good working order. It's the little things that will go a long way toward helping you get top dollar and a quick sale for your property.

If you have any insect damage or rot in the basement, fix it before you show it. You do not want anyone to think that you may have a structural problem. Just the mere insinuation of a structural problem, and your buyers are thinking big bucks and thinking about the next house on their list.

In a nut shell, put a little extra into those kitchens and baths, and anything else you can do to make the new buyer feel more secure. Then you will get top dollar for your home.

# Chapter 11
## The Final Touches

You've got the majority of the rehab done. You're just about ready to start advertising it to the general public. Now take a little time and walk around your property. Think to yourself, "What could I do to this property to make it stand out from every other home that is currently on the market?"

Let's start with curb appeal. When a new buyer pulls up in front of your house, you want it to look as appealing as possible because at this time they are making the decision as to whether or not they are even going to get out of their car!

Many a sale has been lost because, although the inside looks gorgeous, the outside of the house was neglected, and the potential buyer sped right by and onto the next house on their list.

This is what you need to do to make your house stand out:

The yard should be clean of any debris, whether it be trash or leaves that have collected in some corner of the house or yard.

The driveway should be in good condition. (Does it need repair, should you black top it?)

There should be no peeling paint or broken vinyl on the siding, trim or decking. If the paint, siding or decking is dirty, power wash it clean. The gutters should all be intact with no missing down spouts.

The landscaping is very important. Your shrubs should be trimmed. If you have old overgrown shrubs, pull them out and plant new ones. Install a nice landscape design.

Use the "rule of threes" -- three of this and three of that. I usually plant hearty flowers in the shrubbery area to add pleasant colors. If there is

To Get the Forms for This Book and A Free Bonus Gift visit
www.FormsForBook.com

no good spot to plant flowers then I'll add a flower box or a half whiskey barrel planter. If you're not sure what to plant, take the measurements from each side of the front door to the edge of the house -- both the left and right side. Bring the measurements to your local landscape company and they will give you ideas of what you will need. Then put a nice colored mulch down to add to the allure.

If you already have nice landscaping in place, it should be trimmed to look as neat as possible. The yard should be mowed on a regular basis.

The door should be painted a nice warm, inviting color. It should stand out from the color of the house and compliment it nicely. I like to paint my doors a cranberry red, colonial blue or forest green, depending on the color of the house.

If the front of the house does not have shutters, install them. The shutters should match the front door. It may be wise to see what colors are available in the shutters before you choose the color of your door. Since the inexpensive but nice looking shutters are plastic, you can bring the shutter to the paint department and have them match the color with the proper paint. If they can't match it, they can make it. I have gotten plastic shutters in all of the colors that I have previously mentioned.

One exception to the shutters matching the door rule is a for white house with black shutters. A cranberry red door looks great with this combination.

The mailbox, house numbers and the front exterior lighting should all match, whether they are gold, brass or black. If you can, gold or brass looks great.

I always put a fancy door handle on the front door (this can also match the mailbox…if gold or brass). This will be the first thing that the homeowner will touch and will put a positive impression in their minds.

Inside, the house should always be neat and clean. Nobody wants to buy someone else's dirt. The kitchen and bathroom sinks should have new fancy faucets. Use the latest unique designs and you will literally hear the buyer saying, "Ooooooh, look at the faucet." When possible, install a modern sink as well.

The kitchen and bath should be immaculate! Always re-caulk and re-grout the tub/shower if necessary.

As I mentioned previously, I make an older house look more modern by changing all the light switches and outlets to the square modern versions. Of course, I match the switches and outlets with the wall colors or trim, whichever makes the most sense.

Whenever possible, install a ceiling fan instead of a light fixture. This gives the allure of elegance. People love ceiling fans. Change all the light bulbs to the highest, safest wattage possible, and turn on all the lights whenever the house is being shown. This will help the house to appear brighter and more cheery.

Instead of having regular window shades, install blinds. They only cost a couple of dollars more but will enhance the inside of the house. Always leave them in the open position to let as much light into the house a possible; this will help the house appear bigger.

Hardwood floors should always be refinished. If you have hardwood flooring under the carpeting, remove the carpeting (if it is good carpet, save it for another job) and expose them. People love gleaming hardwood floors! And, believe it or not, a lot of people are allergic to carpet.

If the house you are selling has furniture in it, you should make sure that it is not over furnished. You don't want the furniture to look crowded in a room. This will make the house and room look small. If this is the case, simply remove some and either store it in the basement or somewhere off site.

The rule is, the less clutter in the house, the bigger it looks. The more clutter, the more turned off your buyer will be. Remove that clutter!!

When showing a house, you should have scented candles burning throughout and if possible play soft music. If there is a fireplace, get one of those Duraflame-type logs and have a fire going. This creates a soothing and relaxing atmosphere.

Now the stage is set! Sell that house!

# *Chapter 12*
# **Working With Contractors**

Sometimes the most difficult aspect of any renovations job is finding and working with the contractors.

## **Where to Find Contractors**

The best place to find contractors is through a referral of a friend, co-worker, family member or another contractor. These people will refer contractors that have done a good job for them in the past, so at least you have somewhat of a record of performance.

The next best places are the supply stores. Go to the supply stores that electricians, plumbers and carpenters go to get their stock. Ask the people behind the counter which plumbers and electricians have the best reputation and do the best work. They will know. This is the heart of the contractor's existence, and they all talk about who's doing what and what who has done.

Go to the city or town hall in the area in which you will be doing the work. Ask the inspector (plumbing, wiring and/or building) for three names of contractors who he knows who do a lot of work in town. Don't ask him for a referral as he will not be able to refer a particular contractor. But believe me, if you ask for three names, he will give you three guys who do good work and do not give him hassles. This is what you want, because it's these inspectors who will be coming out to the property to sign off on the work. If you're working with a contractor that he doesn't like, he may find additional work (a lot of additional work) that he will require before he signs off on the job.

This is another way of checking a referral. Call the inspector and mention the name of the contractor and ask him if he has had any trouble with him in the past.

To Get the Forms for This Book and A Free Bonus Gift visit
www.FormsForBook.com

The next place to look is the big box stores like Home Depot or Lowe's. A lot of the employees there do the work themselves and have a part-time job at these stores to supplement their income or to get insurance. They also come into contact with a lot of trades' people. Although they do come in contact with them, a referral from these people may be a little riskier since they have not seen their work and have not spoken to their customers.

Every local newspaper has a section in the classified advertisements where trades people advertise. This is good source to find aggressive smaller contractors who usually charge less than the big companies that you may find in the phone book. Always ask for references from past clients when you make contact with them.

Stopping at a job site when you see trucks out front is a way that I have gotten a contractor or two. Not only do you get the chance to meet the contractor, but you also get to view his work.

The last place you want to look is the yellow pages. This is a complete shot in the dark, and you should always check references. I have had good luck and found the plumber who has done most of my work for the last nine years through his ad in the phone book.

## The Bidding Process

You should always get three bids and let the others know that you are getting other bids so that they will sharpen their pencils and give you a good price.

You may have a tendency to jump on the first bid to get the job going. If you are doing this right, you should be getting the bids well before you actually own the house (during the escrow period).

Some contractors are smooth talkers and may pressure you to give them the job that instant. They will make all kinds of promises…but get three bids anyway.

When choosing from the three bids, you may be inclined to choose the lowest bid. Be wary. The lowest bid may be from a contractor that you don't feel comfortable with. Your contractor will become a partner on the job, and you will not be able to complete the job without him. Make sure that you will be able to work with this person. If you have any doubts, don't do it. You will be sorry later. Go with you gut feeling.

Sometimes contractors will give you a low bid in the beginning only to add extras later on. This is called an overage. Let your contractors know up front that you do not expect any overages, and that their bids should reflect any risk of unknown factors up front.

The only time I will allow an overage is when a contractor has to open a wall, remove a covering (shingles), or maybe the ground, and upon opening he finds something in there that he did not expect. This does not happen often, and when it does, I come out to the site, look into the opening and see why he didn't expect what he saw. Then I'll either O.K. or deny the overage. When it is apparent that the overage is fair, then this becomes a change order. I'll explain change orders and how to handle them later.

Electricians are famous for overages. Don't allow it.

After you establish a relationship with a contractor and he has done a couple of jobs for you, you may begin to feel comfortable and trusting and only get his bid for the job. Don't fall into this trap. The more work a contractor does for you the more comfortable he will get with you and the more comfortable he will be to raise his prices. A little at first, and then, before you know it, you're paying top dollar for your repairs.

Keep your contractor honest by always getting at least a second bid.

Your contractors should be fully licensed and insured. Get copies of their license and their insurance. If you don't and someone gets hurt on the job, it will be too late then to find out that your contractor has no insurance and you are the one who is liable.

Make sure that the contractor applies for and gets all necessary permits. You don't want a reputation in the inspection department in your city for being sneaky. When they catch you, and they will eventually catch you, they will come down hard on you, and this will cost you a lot more money in the long run.

Do what the city requires in terms of permits and fees. In the end, a good working relationship with your local building, plumbing and electrical inspectors is the best thing you can do for your company.

# Agreements

### Independent Contractor's Agreement

The first thing that you will want to sign with the contractor who wins the bid is an Independent Contractor's Agreement. This basically states that the contractor is working for himself, independently of you, and that he is not your employee. By doing this, you avoid any employee taxes and establish the proper relationship between yourself and your contractor.

The Independent Contractor Agreement also states that is the responsibility of the contractor to provide his own insurances, both liability and workman's compensation insurance. Don't take their word for it, get a copy of their insurance binders for your records. You would be wise to get the name of their insurance agent and have that agent send you the binders directly. I have had a contractor forge a binder in order to get a job from me. Fortunately, I checked with the insurance company that was listed on the binder and found out that no such policy existed before he was awarded the job.

The last paragraph on the Independent Contractor Agreement has the contractor agree not to hold anyone responsible for any claims or liabilities that may arise from this work, and the contractor agrees to waive any rights that the contractor has to hold anyone liable for any reason as a result of his work. This helps protect you in case one of the contractor's workers or the contractor himself gets hurt on the job and he is not sufficiently covered by his insurances.

Make sure that this agreement is signed.

To Get the Forms for This Book and A Free Bonus Gift visit
www.FormsForBook.com

### Independent Contractor Service Agreement

This is the actual contract between you and the contractor that explains exactly how your business relationship will operate.

Paragraph one again reiterates the relationship between customer and independent contractor. This paragraph does not substitute for the Independent Contractor's Agreement!!

Paragraph two refers to exhibit "A" which describes exactly what the contractor has been contracted to do.

Paragraph three prevents the contractor from hiring someone else to do his work without your permission. There have been times when I have hired a contractor to perform a job and then have gone to the job site to find a crew of guys with another company name on their T-shirts. What the contractor did was sub out the work to another company.

I hired that contractor because I wanted him to perform the work. If he couldn't do it, or if he didn't plan on doing it, he should have consulted with me before he put another company on my job site.

The good thing is that the other company did a really good job and I hired them to do more work for me at a rate less than what I would have paid the other contractor!

This paragraph basically keeps you in control of your job site.

Paragraph four puts the responsibility for obtaining the permit on the contractor. Make sure he obtains all necessary permits and that the permits are posted in the window as per the building code. It would be a good idea to read the permits. On two occasions I have had contractors take a permit off another job and put it in my window!

Ronald Reagan said it best…trust but verify!

To Get the Forms for This Book and A Free Bonus Gift visit
www.FormsForBook.com

Paragraph five has the contractor arrange for all inspections. They will gladly do this when they realize that they will not get paid until the inspector signs off on the job.

Paragraph six lets the contractor know what you expect in terms of a clean job site. Make sure you emphasize this paragraph and that the contractor knows that you expect a clean site at the end of every workday. Make sure that you are on site at the end of the first couple of days to make sure that the contractor is complying with this paragraph. If you don't, before you know it, your job site will look like a dump. Set your expectations, and follow those expectations up with action at the beginning, and your job will run smoother.

Paragraph seven is your start date, end date and penalties if these dates are not met. When running a rehab project, jobs are done in a certain order, and some contractors cannot start until others finish. It's very easy for a negligent contractor to hold up your entire job. This will be your toughest battle when trying to get your job finished. More time is wasted trying to keep a contractor on your job and have him finish in a timely manner than anything else you will do when rehabbing.

This is why we have the penalty clause. If a contractor knows that he will be penalized where it hurts most, in his wallet, he will do whatever it takes to get the job done. Your job will be his top priority.

Paragraph eight will protect you against the contractor doing work and then charging you for it after the fact. It should be spelled out to the contractor that any additional work done, if he wants to be compensated, must be approved in writing, with both your and his signatures **prior** to him doing the work. Otherwise you will consider it a gesture of good will!

I once had a septic contractor hand me a bill at the end of a job for an additional $8,000! He stated that he came across a problem and fixed it. Problem was, he didn't notify me and the problem was underground. While the pit was open he should have called me to explain what he encountered and what needed to be done to rectify it. He didn't. He didn't tell me until after he closed up the hole.

I didn't pay him. He knew that he had to get an O.K. for any extras. He had been in business for over 20 years. There was no reason that he didn't call me, except maybe that the problem wasn't as bad as $8000. I had every right not to pay him and he knew it. I never used him again, and he didn't wave to me anymore when I saw him on the streets. His loss.

Always require a Change Order in writing prior to the start of any additional work.

Paragraph nine refers to Exhibit "B" which is the draw schedule. This tells the contractor how and when he will be paid. I usually do my draws in threes. The initial money is just enough to buy his supplies, any extra and the contractor may be off an running.

Some contractors run their businesses by getting half up front from one job to finance another. Don't do it. Never give half up front. Only give enough for supplies. Even then I will have the contractor call the supply company, have the supply company create a bill and fax it to me. I will review it and then pay for the supplies with my credit card.

When reviewing the list from the supply company, I'm looking for things like tools and odd supplies that may not be needed on my job. I will not pay for these items, and I will ask for an explanation of any odd item. If it looks good, then I'll pay it.

The draws are usually set up to be given when the normal inspections are required with the building, plumbing or electrical inspector. After the inspection is signed off, I'll pay. If no inspections are due, then I will specify at which stages I will pay and exactly what must be completed at each stage in order for the contractor to get paid.

Again, I like to pay in four installments. First payment for supplies, second payment when a certain amount of work is complete, third payment when the next set of work is done, and the last payment for final completion.

Never make a payment until you are satisfied. If you do, you risk the contractor not completing the work! Never, never, never pay a contractor without first inspecting the job. No matter what he says!!! If you do, you will be sorry.

When a contractor calls for an inspection, even though the agreement says you have up to three days to inspect, get out there as soon as possible and bring your checkbook.

You want to treat your contractors like gold. If you have the reputation of making people wait for their money, they will make you wait to get the work done.

If they know that you will pay immediately, they will put other peoples' jobs on hold just to do yours. I know this because this is the secret to how I get my work done so quickly.

So get out there to inspect and write that check!!

Paragraph ten explains the parameters of customer approval. You expect to see the sign-off on the permits and you always work off a punch list so both parties are in agreement as to what needs to be completed.

You need this because when you go to re-inspect and there are still one or two items that need to be completed and the contractor is whining for a payment, you pull out the list that you both signed and ask him why he didn't complete the list.

Paragraph eleven addresses the importance of communication. Many times it has taken days for a contractor to get back to me. It drives me crazy. Paragraph eleven lets them know that if they do not communicate with you, they risk you terminating them from the job.

Paragraph twelve lets you know where the contractor lives. This also lets the contractor know that you know where he lives to help keep him on the up and up. If he knows that you know where he lives, the chances of him disappearing from a job are lowered considerably. If you can't get an address from a contractor, don't do business with him.

Paragraph thirteen allows you to cancel any services that the contractor has yet to perform. You will want this option for two reasons.

To Get the Forms for This Book and A Free Bonus Gift visit
www.FormsForBook.com

First, if after the contractor has done some of the work, you realize that he does not perform to a level that you would like then you can let him go.

Second, if he does not complete the work in a timely manner, you will want to move on to someone who will.

Paragraph fourteen allows you to act outside of the contract and not jeopardize the agreement, meaning if you do something differently than what was spelled out in one of the paragraphs in the contact, this doesn't mean that the entire contract has ended.

Paragraph fifteen is one more way to protect you against any costly or frivolous lawsuits.

People have a tendency to award a contractor a job and not have the contractor sign the agreements. This is a big mistake. This contract will protect you from a number of costly pitfalls that have the potential of happening during your relationship with your contractor.

Not only that, but the contract establishes the type of relationship and the parameters of that relationship that you will have with your contractor. You will look and be more professional and be treated as such.

## Exhibit "A" Scope of Work

This form is a part of every Independent Contractor's Service Agreement. This specifies exactly what work is to be done.

When filling out this form, be as detailed as possible. If you have a disagreement with a contractor about how a job should have been completed, you should be able to go back to this document and show him exactly how he differs from what was agreed upon on the Scope of Work exhibit.

I always add the following sentence at the end of my Scope of Work exhibit, "Contractor to perform all work in compliance with all state and local building codes."

This puts the burden solely on the contractor to perform up to inspectional standards.

Here are some items that you will want to specify when completing the Scope of Work for certain jobs:

Roofing

Type of material
Grade of material (i.e. 25 year asphalt shingles)
Who hauls away the shingles?
Tarping off the roof (to be done at the end of every day)
Tarping off the ground, to protect the shrubs
If roof decking is required, what is the price per square foot to replace?

Painting

Grade of paint
Number of coats
Amount of wall prep expected (contractor shall prepare the surface of the walls so that they are smooth throughout the house)
Manufacturer and color of paint
Clean up

Windows

Style of window (i.e. vinyl clad, insulated windows)
Grids (if any)
Quantity

Carpet/Lino

Grade of carpet/lino
Grade of pad
Color of carpet/lino
If lino, sub-floor if necessary
How the sub-floor is to be nailed off

Heating/Air

Type of system

To Get the Forms for This Book and A Free Bonus Gift visit
www.FormsForBook.com

Number of BTU's (make sure that this is in
compliance with local codes)
Who will be responsible for any electrical work?
Is duct work required?

Doors

Style
Material
Placement (what goes where)
Does contractor supply and install the new
handsets?

Appliances

Style (self cleaning oven, gas/electric)
Color
Who is responsible for any plumbing or electrical
work?

Ceiling Fixtures

Color
Style
Quantity

## Modification Agreement, Change Order

There will come a time when a contractor comes to you and tells
you that he will have to do something different than what the original
agreement called for, or you may change your mind and want something
done in a different way.

When this happens, always, always, always put the change in
writing so that both you and the contractor agree upon exactly what is
going to be changed and how it will affect the price of the job. Make sure
both parties sign the change order.

## Damage Clause

The damage clause puts your contractor on notice that he and his
employees are responsible for any damage that they do to either existing
conditions or to new work performed by other contactors.

To Get the Forms for This Book and A Free Bonus Gift visit
www.FormsForBook.com

This happens a lot. People are just plain careless and do damage to other parts of house while they are doing their work. Be prepared to exercise this clause.

You have the option of either using that contractor to perform the work or having another contractor do the job. Regardless of who does it, your contractor will know that he is expected to reimburse you either monetarily, or with repairs, for any damage that he or his workers do.

### Notice of Termination

When a contractor simply won't live up to the agreement that he signed and has become an obstacle for you getting the job done, or his work is just not of the quality that you can allow, terminate him.

If you think that you may have to terminate a contractor, plan ahead. You will want to have another contractor waiting in the wings ready to come in and complete the job. If you don't, you should continue to try to work with your current contractor until you find a replacement; otherwise your job will sit idle. If you are at least still trying to work with the current one, you may get some sort of progress. You know the old saying…don't cut off your nose to spite your face!

When you send this letter of termination, send it certified mail. This will give you proof that he received it in case he decides to show up on the job site pretending that all is well. It also gives you evidence to show the court in the event that a lawsuit comes about.

Don't be afraid to terminate bad contractors. It's your profit that's at stake!

### Contractor Punch Out List

When the contractor requests a disbursement, whether it be the first, second, third, or last, you need to inspect the job and make sure that everything is done the way it is supposed to be done.

If it's not, take out your Punch Out List and write down everything that was supposed to be done and is not. Go over the list with the contractor, explain to him what needs to be done before you can pay him, and have him sign the form.

To Get the Forms for This Book and A Free Bonus Gift visit
www.FormsForBook.com

Make sure you go over exactly what you expect to be completed. I have had contractors drag me out to a job site two or three times and still not have everything on the list done when I got there. These are usually not the best people to be working with, but nonetheless, you will meet several contractors who will do this.

Before I go out the second time, I will tell the contractor that I expect the list to be 100 percent completed or the next time I have to come out it will take me a long time to get there. Of course I say this as pleasantly as possible. Nobody likes a hard ass. Translation-let's not screw around. My time is valuable and your paycheck is on the line.

They usually get the message.

Do not pay that final disbursement until you are 100 percent satisfied that all the items on the punch out list have been completed. If you do, you will have a hard time getting that contactor back onto the site.

### Lien Waiver

Each time you make a payment to a contractor, get a lien waiver signed. This is like a receipt. If for some reason the contractor unjustly puts a mechanics lien or has justly put a mechanics lien on your property, you simply go to the courthouse and record the lien waiver, and your title will become clear.

A mechanics lien is what is used in the trades to let the public know that work performed was on a property that hasn't been paid for. A tradesman will produce a mechanics lien and record it against the property at the registry of deeds. Until the lien has been satisfied, the house cannot be sold. Sometimes they do not tell you that they have placed a mechanics lien on the property. This is why it is important to have a lien waiver signed each time you make a payment to a contractor.

# Rehab Timelines

| | |
|---|---|
| Interior paint (basic prep, prime, paint) | *1.5 weeks – 1,500 square foot house* |
| Install an interior door | *1 hour* |
| Install a pre-hung interior door | *1.5 hours* |
| Install a pre-hung exterior door | *4 hours* |
| Install kitchen cabinets | *2 days – basic 12' set* |
| Install counter tops, sink, faucet | *4 – 8 hours* |
| Windows | *½ hour per window* |
| Vinyl siding | *5 days – 1,500 square foot house* |
| Gutters | *4 hours – 1,500 square foot house, 2 sides* |
| Shutters | *½ hour per window* |
| Electrical panel upgrade | *1 day* |
| Electrical entire upgrade | *4 days* |
| Toilet replace | *1 hour* |
| Grout/caulk tub | *4 hours* |
| Install vanity, sink and faucet | *4 hours* |
| Install tub | *1 day* |
| Replace heating system | *1 day* |
| Install new heating system | *3 days* |

| | |
|---|---|
| Exterior paint | *4 – 5 days, 1,500 square foot house* |
| Roof – overlay | *3 days, 1,500 square foot house* |
| Roof – strip | *5 days, 1,500 square foot house* |
| Carpet | *2 days, 5 rooms and hall* |
| Vinyl floor | *1 day, kitchen and bath* |
| Hardwood floors | *4 days, sanding and two coats of poly* |
| Tile floor | *3 days – kitchen and bath* |
| Landscaping | *4 hours* |

# *Chapter 13*

# **Renovation Management**

When performing rehabs on your houses, you'll want to use different systems to track your progress. The more systems you have, the better off you'll be and the more in control you'll be of your deals.

The more in control you are, the more rehabs that you will be able to do at any given time. The more rehabs you do, the more money you will make. The importance of systems and how they make you wealthy is explained fully in Michael Gerber's book *The E-Myth Revisited*. It's an excellent book, you should read it.

## **Accounting**

The first thing you will want to do is to set up an accounting system. Quickbooks software is an excellent accounting program and has all of the features that you will need to run your jobs. I have been using it for over seven years now. There are other good ones out there but I think this one is the most user-friendly.

If you're the type that likes to use pencil and paper, then go to you local office supply store and get some accounting paper and set up a log. I have enclosed a Rehab Accounting Log that you can use as an example.

You want to track the following information:

- ✓ The date of the expense
- ✓ Who you paid
- ✓ What you paid for
- ✓ What it went to (if it needs an explanation)
- ✓ How you paid for it
- ✓ How much it was
- ✓ A running total of your expenses

To Get the Forms for This Book and A Free Bonus Gift visit
www.FormsForBook.com

It is important that you write down everything, and write it down either the day of the expense or the morning after. If you're like me and you put off writing down the expense, before you know it, you have forgotten about something and then it's not accounted for. Do this a few times and your costs are out of whack.

It's important to keep track of your expenses for two reasons. The first is to make sure that you are within budget. Then if you are starting to go out of budget, you can take measures to put yourself back in line. In the beginning, when I didn't track my expenses diligently, my jobs would come in $5,000, $10,000 and $15,000 over budget!! It's very easy to go over budget, and it's very easy to lose all of your profit on a job. By tracking all of your expenses, you know where you stand at any given time.

The second reason to track expenses is so you can see what things actually cost, compared to what you estimated. You can use this information when estimating other jobs so that your estimates are more accurate, thus making each job more profitable.

# Planning

You are going to want to plan your jobs from start to finish. I have developed a couple of forms that I use to plan my jobs. The first is the overall Job Schedule sheet. At a glance, I can look at my job on paper, from start to finish and know who should be on my site and when they should be finished.

The chart is broken down into weekly intervals.

The guides that you will need when planning your jobs are the Planning Repairs Quick Guide and the Rehab Timelines. The Planning Repairs Quick Guide will show you what order the jobs need to be done in. The Rehab Timeline lets you know how long you should expect each job to take so that you can plan accordingly.

On the Rehab Planning Schedule, you'll see that I have two boxes under the job description. These are for planned start and completion dates, and actual start and completion dates. Everything is always written in pencil because this schedule will change. I have not had a single job that went from the beginning to the end without a change on the Job Schedule sheet.

You can see that certain jobs cannot start until others have ended. If a contractor in one of these key slots does not complete his work on time, the rest of the schedule has to be changed and each contractor has to be notified.

You can look at the chart in a glance and know which contractors you have to call to make sure that they are going to be on the job on time, or which contractors you have to inform of a delay.

As each assignment is done, it gets checked off until all of the items are checked off and your house is complete.

## Activities Worksheet

The Activities Worksheet is completed before you fill out the Rehab Planning Schedule. This is where you list all of the contractors, suppliers, utility companies and whoever else you will need to contact in order for this job to be completed.

You may fill out many Activity Worksheets for a single job because if you need many contractors to complete the job, you will have to contact many more because you will be getting at least three bids for each job. This is where you track who you need to call and when they are to perform a task for you (get you the bid, turn on the gas, etc.).

This is also where you put the tasks that will be performed by you as the job progresses.

For instance, in our example at 10 Hunt Street, you can see on the sheet that I have listed all of the contractors that I plan to get into the property to get bids. I list who they are and what they are bidding on and give myself a due date. This ensures that I have all my bids in before my closing date so that I can get the job done as soon as possible.

If you spend an hour a day planning your day, week, month and year, you will have a business -- and a life -- that will reap you greater and greater rewards. The biggest mistake that most people make in their lives and careers is failing to plan.

It's a lot like goal setting. You're spending each day planning how that day will turn out. If you don't, before you know it the day is over and although you were very busy, you didn't get anything accomplished.

Planning is one of the hardest things to do consistently until it becomes a habit. As I mentioned earlier, to plan consistently is like trying to make an oil tanker turn 180 degrees in the open ocean.

A ship that big takes almost two miles to make a full turn. With everything that has been ingrained into you throughout all of your years and all of the habits that you have developed, learning to plan consistently takes time and commitment to master. But once you've made the turn, you will achieve things that you once thought unimaginable!!

So plan every day, and when a couple of days go by and you haven't spent time planning, don't get discouraged, start again the next day. Keep doing this, and with this attitude you will get to where you want to be, which is planning consistently.

## Communications

The Contractor/Job Site Communications Log allows you to keep track of all of the communications that you will use with your contractor and any other individuals (city inspectors, attorneys, insurance agents, buyers, etc.) regarding your job site.

If there is ever a discrepancy as to what you spoke to any particular individual about, you will have what and when you talked about in writing. This form once saved me an insurance claim on a property a while ago. Since I do so many rehabs, I use the same insurance agency with whom I have built a good relationship with over the years.

After I submitted the claim, my agent called with the bad news. He said I had never requested insurance for this particular house. I went back

To Get the Forms for This Book and A Free Bonus Gift visit
www.FormsForBook.com

to my Contractor/Job Site Communications Log and showed him that I had called on a specific date and talked with his secretary and ordered the insurance. It was obvious that she made the mistake, and he personally paid the claim.

This form also allows you keep track of who you called and when you called them. Sometimes you will call several different contractors for bids for a property and no bids come back. So it's time to call back the contractors and find out where the bids are, or call other contractors to get more bids.

After calling so many contractors for a certain job, you're not sure who you have called and who you haven't. This form, if filled out properly, will tell who you called and when you called them.

Keeping track of all of this information will give you the ability to run more and more jobs simultaneously.

# Rehab Accounting Log

Property
Address_____

Start date _____          Completed Date _____

| Date: | Paid To: | Description: | Method Of Payment | Amount Of Payment | Running Total: |
|-------|----------|--------------|-------------------|-------------------|----------------|
|       |          |              |                   |                   |                |
|       |          |              |                   |                   |                |
|       |          |              |                   |                   |                |
|       |          |              |                   |                   |                |
|       |          |              |                   |                   |                |
|       |          |              |                   |                   |                |
|       |          |              |                   |                   |                |
|       |          |              |                   |                   |                |
|       |          |              |                   |                   |                |
|       |          |              |                   |                   |                |
|       |          |              |                   |                   |                |
|       |          |              |                   |                   |                |
|       |          |              |                   |                   |                |
| **TOTAL:** |     |              |                   |                   |                |

# Rehab Planning Schedule

Property Address _____
Start Date _____

| Description | | Week Of: | Week Of: | Week Of: | Week Of: | Week Of: | Week Of: | Week Of: | Week Of: |
|---|---|---|---|---|---|---|---|---|---|
| | Plan | | | | | | | | |
| | Act | | | | | | | | |
| | Plan | | | | | | | | |
| | Act | | | | | | | | |
| | Plan | | | | | | | | |
| | Act | | | | | | | | |
| | Plan | | | | | | | | |
| | Act | | | | | | | | |
| | Plan | | | | | | | | |
| | Act | | | | | | | | |
| | Plan | | | | | | | | |
| | Act | | | | | | | | |
| | Plan | | | | | | | | |
| | Act | | | | | | | | |
| | Plan | | | | | | | | |
| | Act | | | | | | | | |
| | | | | | | | | | |

# Rehab Activities Worksheet

Property Address_____

| Activity | Due Date | Comments |
|---|---|---|
|  |  |  |
|  |  |  |
|  |  |  |
|  |  |  |
|  |  |  |
|  |  |  |
|  |  |  |
|  |  |  |
|  |  |  |
|  |  |  |
|  |  |  |
|  |  |  |
|  |  |  |
|  |  |  |
|  |  |  |
|  |  |  |
|  |  |  |
|  |  |  |

# Contractor/Job Site Communications Log

Job Site _____

| Spoke With: | Date: | Comments: |
|---|---|---|
| | | |
| | | |
| | | |
| | | |
| | | |
| | | |
| | | |
| | | |
| | | |
| | | |
| | | |
| | | |
| | | |
| | | |
| | | |
| | | |
| | | |
| | | |

# Chapter 14

# Taking The Next Step

At this point, you may now realize that there is a lot of money to be made in the real estate investment game. I quickly learned, at the start of my real estate investing career, the more I learn the more I earn.

If you would like additional resources or if you would like a personal coach to help you reach your real estate goals faster, you can contact us at the office at 781-878-7114.

You are about to embark on a journey that can create financial freedom for you and your family and it can happen in a very short period of time.

Call us when you are having difficulties and we will help you break through your obstacles. Call us when you accomplish your triumphs and we will celebrate with you!!!

Here at the Creative Success Alliance, we now consider you a part of the family and we are here to support you during this wondrous journey of real estate investing!!

To Get the Forms for This Book and A Free Bonus Gift visit
www.FormsForBook.com